TEEN SPIRIT

For Mom.

The author respectfully acknowledges the following writers and journalists, whose works proved to be an invaluable resource:
Lorraine Ali, Gina Arnold, Michael Azerrad, Gavin Edwards, Jason Fine, David Fricke, Mikal Gilmore, Joe Gore, Robert Hilburn, Clark Humphrey, Mark Kemp, Chris Mundy, Christopher Sandford, and Eric Weisbard
Special thanks to Jon Auer, Robert Hilburn, Harvey Kubernik, and Kyra Thompson.
And a very large thank you to Kurt, for the songs, and Nirvana, for the music.

Picture acknowledgements
The publishers would like to thank the following sources for their kind permission to reproduce the pictures in this book:
All Action/Justin Thomas; **Corbis-Bettmann**/Reuter, UPI; **Hulton Getty**;
London Features International/Matt Anker, Kristin Callahan, Kevin Mazur, Derek Ridgers; **Redferns**/Mick Hutson, Max Jones Files;
Retna Pictures/Matt Anker, Charlie Hoselton, Alastair Indge, Niels Van Iperen, Steve Pyke, Ed Sirrs, Stephen Sweet, Chris Taylor, Ian T Tilton, Alice Wheeler; **Rex Features**/LGI Photo Agency/Carlos Arthur, John Mantel, SIPA, Today, Kirk Weddle, Jeff Werner; **Science Photo Library**/John Burbidge, Adam Hart-Davis, Mehau Kulyk; **S.I.N.**/David Anderson, Richard Beland, Steve Double, Martyn Goodacre, Jayne Houghton, Alastair Indge, Jana, Tim Owen, Roy Tee, Ian T Tilton.
Every effort has been made to acknowledge correctly and contact the source and/or copyright holder of each picture, and Carlton Books Limited apologises for any unintentional errors or omissions which will be corrected in future editions of this book.

Fireside
Rockefeller Center
1230 Avenue of the Americas
New York, New York 10020

Printed and bound in Great Britain

THIS IS A CARLTON BOOK

10 9 8 7 6 5 4 3 2 1

Cataloging-in-Publication Data is available from
the Library of Congress

ISBN 0-684-83356-5

Executive Editor: Lorraine Dickey
Editor: Mike Flynn
Art Editor: Vicky Harvey
Design: Norma Martin
Picture Research: Emily Hedges
Production: Sarah Schuman

TEEN SPIRIT

THE STORIES BEHIND EVERY NIRVANA SONG

CHUCK CRISAFULLI

A Fireside Book
Published by Simon & Schuster

CONTENTS

introduction...

It was teen spirit that rescued rock n' roll. The music was in a sad shape as it rolled into the 1990s; tired, tamed and trivialized. Pop-charts were bloated with puffy, synthesized, made-for-market fluff. Glam-metal, which sounded energizing for a second or two in the late 1980s, had already collapsed into a clownish, overwrought bore. Punk rock was exhausted and the underground was splintered into dozens of unfocused, largely unheard, scenes. Great music – great rock n' roll – was still out there, to be sure, and one could track it down record by record. But rock n' roll as urgent life-force, as vital celebration, as the music of fierce community – that rock n' roll had gone very, very quiet. It was in need of rescue, but who would turn the guitars back up?

Salvation came in an unlikely form, and from an unexpected place: an awesome blast of dread and distortion from the American Northwest.

September, 1991.

hello, nirvana.

Only a handful of rock n' roll records had ever announced themselves as instant signposts; loudly, cleanly marking pop history into a "before" and "after." *Sgt. Pepper* was one of those, as was *Never Mind the Bollocks Here's the Sex Pistols*. When Nirvana released *Nevermind*, they issued rock's next grand directive. And it pointed the way toward once more making the music sweaty, ugly, smart, funny, consuming, necessary and loud. This humble trio in flannel reclaimed rock n' roll's past and re-established its future. In consummate fashion, they kicked ass and opened minds.

Nirvana's music heralded a revolution but, separated into its component parts, the band's sound was not really revolutionary. Catchy melodies, sing-along choruses, anguished howls, cranked guitars – these had been the basic, primal ingredients to just about every great band's sound. But the mix here was fresh, inspired and inspiring, and what was entirely new was the spirit. Never before had brute force sounded so sweet, and never before had pop constructions carried so much fearsome weight. The brilliant simplicity and simple brilliance of Kurt Cobain's songs made genius sound easy, but there certainly was genius there – slouch, shrug, scowl and stumble as it might.

Nirvana's greatest accomplishment was in making old rock n' roll – retrograde beast that it is – shiver and spasm into a thoroughly modern statement of purpose. They made a heap of pop-culture contradictions sound not only invigorating but righteous: pop tunes were punk, punk was pop, noise was beautiful, angst was celebration, apathy was communion and a chunk of the underground could simply up and conquer the mainstream. Rock n' roll smelled like teen spirit, and never smelled better.

Bottom line: in its short history, Nirvana never stopped making thrilling sounds. Bleach was an ear-singing warning shot, *Nevermind* a pop manifesto and *In Utero* a rousing mega-rant. All three, along with *Incesticide* and *Unplugged*, hold up as potent, original works that, at their finest moments, make a listener feel fully alive – the way all great rock n' roll does. Kurt Cobain was a troubled and fragile soul, but he was also an inspiring and talented artist, and his small, powerful legacy of work will no doubt continue to shape the sounds around us for years to come.

It is unfortunate and saddening beyond words that Cobain chose to leave us so soon. He will be deeply missed. All we can do is hold on to what he left for us: the songs, the songs, the songs...

Nirvana's story begins in the humblest of places: Aberdeen – a small, gray, forgotten lumber town in the middle of Washington State's outer coast. Aberdeen was once a destination of choice. Years and years ago, when the lumber business was booming and the seaport of Grays Harbor was more active, the town was home to a formidable number of profitable whorehouses. But these days the lumber business is a shadow of what it once was, the local economy is perennially depressed and for a long time the prostitution has been a dimly remembered bit of less-than-glorious civic history. Life in Aberdeen is simple and hard. Taverns fill up early in the day and, if one doesn't drink, there's not much else to do around town. The local suicide rate is well above the US average. In a town so geared to basic subsistence, a sensitive soul is a misfit, and it seems pretty clear that Kurt Cobain grew up painfully aware that he did not fit in.

Cobain was born on February 20, 1967, in Hoquiam, just outside of Aberdeen. He was the first-born son of Wendy and Donald. (Donald was an auto-mechanic.) Kurt enjoyed a contented, unspectacular childhood in Aberdeen, but in 1975 his parents split up and he was never quite comfortable at home again. He bounced between stretches of residence with each parent, feeling like an unwanted stranger in either's house. School was no refuge – Cobain showed promise and interest in his art classes, but otherwise was an unremarkable student who was tagged a weak one - a "faggot" – by rougher, stronger kids. Cobain was well aware, early on, that he was not well suited for a life of convention in Aberdeen.

He found sanctuary in rock n' roll. He spent

Rock n' roll smelled like teen spirit, and never smelled better

hours alone in whatever bedroom he could lay claim to, chopping away at an electric guitar and working up decent version of AC/DC's 'Back in Black' and Led Zeppelin's 'Communication Breakdown.' He began hanging around the rehearsals of a local band, the Melvins. The group's spirited leader, Buzz Osborne, saw fit to turn young Cobain on to the pleasures of the angriest, most splenetic punk rock he had available. Cobain listened intently and repeatedly to compilation tapes Osborne gave him – full of the sounds of Black Flag, Flipper, MDC, the Sex Pistols and the Butthole Surfers. It was a revelation. In the fury, the volume, the do-it-yourself exorcism of punk, Cobain saw a way out of his unhappiness, and maybe even out of Aberdeen. He saw a place where he might fit in. He wanted to be in a band.

One other friend of Buzz Osborne and the Melvins was a lanky fellow named Chris Novoselic (who would later revert to the spelling of his name as it appeared on his birth certificate – Krist Novoselic.) Chris, the son of Croatian immigrants, was born on May 16, 1965, in Compton, California. He spent his early childhood in Southern California, moving to Aberdeen with his family when he was fourteen. Chris too was a lover of Led Zeppelin, along with some Aerosmith and Black Sabbath, and while in high school started playing an electric guitar along to his favorite records. Then – thanks again to Buzz Osborne's compilation tapes – Novoselic underwent the same punk rock conversion that Cobain had. After that, playing along with records just wasn't as satisfying. He wanted to be in a band.

Novoselic's younger brother, Robert, had befriended Kurt. When he brought Kurt to the family's house one afternoon, Cobain heard the unmistakable sounds of crude, punk-rock guitar being hacked out in an upstairs bedroom. He remembered that sound months later – after he'd used an aunt's four-track recorder to put together his first demo tape of original tunes with a friend named Greg Hokanson on drums and Melvins drummer Dale Crover playing bass. Cobain was proud of the work that this trio, dubbed Fecal Matter, had produced and made a point of getting a copy to his friend Robert's older, punk-guitar-playing brother, Chris. When Cobain handed the tape over to Chris and mentioned that the two of them should get a band together, Novoselic shrugged it off and it was a while before he bothered to listen to the Fecal Matter cassette. When he did, he heard something that told him Cobain was right. The next time he ran into Kurt, they agreed to get a band together.

Before the hype: thrashy guitars and flannel shirts were a naturally grungy way of life for early Nirvana.

bleach, released in June 1989, was the roar that only a handful heard. It was a very respectful handful – at a time when the indie/alternative rock scene had no muscle in the market-place, the record exceeded all expectations by selling 30,000 copies over two years. But the record's well-chiseled punk-metal fury hardly heralded the Nirvanamania that was to come. After *Bleach*, every Nirvana album would be an event – a grand dispatch to be scrutinized, analyzed, celebrated and/or vilified. But the band's first full-length release enjoyed the comfort of simply being a very good album from a mostly unknown band.

The album served as something of a metal exorcism for Cobain as a song writer. The record is packed with riffs that owe some debt to all those Black Sabbath and Black Flag tapes that Buzz Osborne from the Melvins had turned Cobain on to, and there are only a few hints, as in 'About A Girl', of the pop craftsmanship that Cobain would soon put to use. Lyrically, the songs on *Bleach* reveal what would become an enduring Cobain trademark – a bent toward meaningful meaninglessness. Listeners attempting to decipher the message behind 'Sifting' – just like listeners later trying to suss out 'Smells Like Teen Spirit' – could understandably be driven to cries of, "What is he talking about?" But while Cobain seemed to be mumbling nonsense – what he might not communicate in cogent narrative was more than clear in the intensity of delivery.

Some of the songs on *Bleach* sound like an understandable testing of the song writing waters for Cobain – the one-note joke of a song such as 'Floyd the

bleach

Barber' almost registers as a Nirvana novelty tune now. But the strength and confidence of the music on *Bleach* tend to disguise the fact that at the time of its creation Cobain was a penniless, sometimes homeless drop-out, racked with self-doubts and uncertainties about his future. Actually, a good deal of the record's driving energy comes from the way Cobain and the band can turn dread and hopelessness into exultation. Being a 'Negative Creep' is nothing to be thrilled about, but the way the band bashed out that song's dumpy feelings made it a weird cry of personal triumph and self-loathing at one and the same time.

Quite soon, Cobain would be assured enough as a writer to examine himself even more closely and make himself extremely vulnerable in his songs, but on *Bleach* – admissions to being a creep notwithstanding – he tended to create

characters ('Mr. Moustache') or scenarios ('School') that offered a bit of cover.

As a band, Nirvana was just beginning to coalesce when recording for *Bleach* began. Cobain and Novoselic had quickly realized that they enjoyed working together. They first began playing together in 1986 (in a space above Novoselic's mom's beauty shop), but direction, and a solid drummer, were harder to come by. In early 1987, the two had begun rehearsing with a drummer named Aaron Burckhard, and it was with him that they played their first gigs in Olympia and Tacoma, under such names as Skid Row, Ted Ed Fred, Bliss, the Sellouts, Pen Cap Chew, Throat Oyster and Windowpane. Finally, with its ironic implications in mind,

Clean needles: Nirvana's first album was named after an anti-AIDS campaign's advice to intravenous drug users.

Post-punk, proto-grunge and decidedly pre-'Teen Spirit': Nirvana's first album was a dark, cramped slab of raging discontents.

Pay to play: Jason Everman bankrolled *Bleach* but wasn't on the record.

hand a copy of the tape over to Sub Pop co-owner Jonathan Poneman. Poneman also liked what he heard, and shortly thereafter asked the band if they would be interested in putting out a single on Sub Pop.

They were, but finding a permanent drummer was a continuing problem as the band gigged around Olympia, Tacoma and Seattle. Crover had moved to San Francisco with the Melvins. A replacement he suggested, Dave Foster, didn't work out, and a second round with Burckhard was unsatisfactory. Finally, Cobain and Novoselic drafted Bainbridge Island native Chad Channing to hold down the beat. With Channing, the band returned to Reciprocal on June 11, 1988, to record the 'Love Buzz'/'Big Cheese' single.

The band continued to play out, to write, and to rehearse, and in December and January 1989 spent more time at Reciprocal with Endino to record the rest of the album. Studio time cost the band just over $600, which Sub Pop was not going to front and which Cobain, Novoselic and Channing couldn't cover. But, anticipating the record's release and an ensuing club tour, the trio had decided to take on a second guitarist, a player named Jason Everman.

Everman put up the money, and was credited as part of the band on the sleeve of *Bleach*, although he hadn't played a note on the record.

With recording finished, the foursome did begin a West Coast tour in February 1989. The album was still untitled at that point, but during a stay in San Francisco, the band took note of a strong, ubiquitous public health campaign designed to fight the spread of AIDS by advising intravenous drug users to clean their needles thoroughly with bleach. Bleach was being dispensed as part of a clean needle exchange program, and the band even spotted a guy downtown dressed up as a bleach bottle in order to spread the bleach message. Having found a way to call up images of cleanliness, filth, health and disease in one simple word, the band went with it. *Bleach*, the album, came out that June.

Speaking of that period to journalist Gina Arnold in a 1992 *Option* magazine article, Novoselic recalled, "We didn't know anything about Sub Pop. We just loved playing. It's just so totally fun. It was the most important thing in my life at the time. It was awesome."

Cobain decided to go with Nirvana. (These implications were made clearer in the song 'Paper Cuts'.) The name stuck, although the band would eventually have to settle copyright suits with a pair of other Nirvanas.

The band's first demo was recorded with Burckhard – a taped radio show for the college station in Olympia – but when Burckhard tired of the number of rehearsals that his bandmates insisted on, they turned to their friend from the Melvins, drummer Dale Crover, and asked if he would help them record a proper demo. Crover agreed, and on January 23, 1988, the band spent a day recording at Reciprocal Recordings studio in Seattle with the help of producer Jack Endino (born Michael Giacondino). Of the 10 songs recorded that day, three – 'Floyd the Barber', 'Paper Cuts' and 'Downer' – ended up on *Bleach*, while another four turned up on *Incesticide*.

Cobain began sending off the demo to the small record labels he was aware of – Chicago's Touch&Go, San Francisco's Alternative Tentacles and Southern California's SST. He didn't send a copy to the budding mini-label closest to him – Seattle's Sub Pop. But Endino was impressed enough with that day's work to

blew

Many of what would become the distinguishing features of Nirvana songs were loudly introduced by the first 3-minute blast on *Bleach* – in a song called 'Blew'. The tune boasted a molten bass and guitar riff that carried the weight of the heaviest heavy metal and the darker menace of punk. It was built of exhilarating, almost shocking dynamic shifts – with Cobain's vocals jumping from the lazy snarl of the first verse to the acid-gargle holler of the choruses. And for all the noisy, booming, low-end abandon of the track, the melody was impossibly catchy and the harmonies pop-sweet. Finally, setting a potent lyrical prototype, the tune sounded impassioned, detached, ironic, post-ironic and funny all at once, while its precise meaning remained nearly indecipherable upon repeated listenings.

Cobain shrugged off the possibilities of deep meaning in any of the *Bleach* tracks, remarking on more than one occasion that the words were simply cobbled together to have something to sing, and that there was little personal meaning in the lyrics. But, as would often be the case, he tended to downplay his gift for deceptively simple insight. It is true that not much gets said in 'Blew', but a large part of the song's power comes from its ability to suggest several sizeable themes with just a few simple words. The singer addresses some confining person, place or thing and requests the right "to blow," "to lose," "to breathe" – each request beginning ever-so-politely with an, "If you wouldn't mind." Cobain's desultory delivery makes these lines ring large – he may be singing to Aberdeen, to his family or to a real or imagined girlfriend. The specifics don't seem important – what comes through is the frustrated ache of someone who wants to escape a bad day or an ugly situation, but who also realizes that his half-hearted complaints will do little to bring about any liberation. The song's coda, "you could do anything," ends up sounding more like an apathetic taunt than a promise of hope.

It is worth remembering that on the most practical level all Kurt really wanted was a few cool words to holler. No respectable punk would slave over internal rhyme schemes and extended conceits, would he? So, Cobain counted on the pressures of recording deadlines for inspiration – scribbling out the final version of 'Blew' on the night before the *Bleach* sessions, when he and the band spent the night at Jason Everman's house in Seattle. An earlier version of the lyrics from one of Kurt's notebooks had some additional lines – the song began as an odd, loveless confrontation set in a garden – but these don't shed any light on the specifics of the song's genesis. Of the lines that were recorded, a telling change was made from the earlier version. Cobain's glumly complacent "I would like to lose" had originally been the more hopeful "I would like to choose."

Some of heavy-bottomed vibe on 'Blew' was accidental. The band had been experimenting with tuning the bass and the guitar down a step for a bigger sound – using what's called a "drop D" tuning, wherein the lowest note on each instrument becomes a D rather than an E. Before recording 'Blew', Kurt and Krist had tuned down, but then forgot they'd done so. When they tuned down again, they accidentally created the sound that gives 'Blew' its distinctive, threatening rumble.

Krist Novoselic's basslines did much to steer Nirvana's sound.

floyd the barber

it's inevitably described by fans as homespun, gentle-spirited and endearing, but perhaps no other show in television history has presented as blindly inane a view of American small-town life as *The Andy Griffith Show*, the show that gave life to the character of Floyd the Barber. The show ran from 1960 to 1968, playing like a tonic to the conservative-minded masses as the decade tumbled tumultuously along. As American notions of sex, drugs, war, money, faith and community were questioned, challenged and transformed, *The Andy Griffith Show* offered a view of an unchanged rural America in which a big event was a trip to the fishing hole or a slice of a freshly baked pie. This entirely manufactured vision of the country's good ol' days was immensely popular, and for the length of its run the show was placed among the top ten programs according to the industry-worshipped Nielsen ratings.

The show was set in Mayberry, North Carolina, but its audience never had to worry about being disturbed by prickly questions of race relations in the American south – blacks, Jews, hippies, free-thinkers and any other unacceptable outsiders never seemed to make it within the town limits. The residents were completely white, polite, undoubtedly Christian and – it might appear to uncharmed eyes – mildly retarded. Town barber Floyd, portrayed by actor Howard McNair, was one of Mayberry's dimmer bulbs. Along with Deputy Barney Fife, loveable town drunk Otis Campbell and a gas-pumper named Goober, Floyd was used for brief scenes of ostensible comic relief, while the main story lines revolved around Sheriff Andy Taylor (played by Griffith), his son Opie (the result of some unexplained procreative act) and Andy's bulldoggish Aunt Bee.

Kurt Cobain was well-acquainted with American

Cobain was not charmed, or accepted, by small-town minds.

Just a little off the top? Small-towners were objects of fear and loathing in 'Floyd the Barber'.

small-town life, and in no way did the goings-on in Aberdeen match up with anything presented in Mayberry. In Aberdeen, the drunks weren't loveable, the dim bulbs were likely to be armed and angry rather than goofily helpful and the community spirit – far from, "Have another slice of pie, won't cha?" – was one of embittered hopelessness. No surprise then, that in one of the first songs he wrote for Nirvana, he put his dark humor to use in turning the homely fantasy of Mayberry into a bloody nightmare.

The song finds poor Kurt in search of a shave, but when he enters Floyd's shop and the barber commences his art, things quickly turn ugly. The singer is tied to the barber chair by the semi-spastic Deputy Fife, is sliced by Opie and Aunt Bee and finally dies at the hands of the Sheriff. Cobain's understated lyrical approach served him well here – instead of going for all-out gore value, the way punk heroes like Flipper or the Butthole Surfers might, Cobain sketches out the murderous scene with just a few incisive phrases.

It is also possible that Kurt – who had strong interests in drawing and painting – may have seen a comic-strip parody of *The Andy Griffith Show* by Drew and Josh Alan Friedman. The strip originally appeared in the artsy, New York-based *Raw* magazine in 1978. In that version of the rural nightmare, Barney and Andy jump away from Aunt Bee's dinner table with news of the appearance of Mayberry's first black visitor. One lynching later, they can sit down to a relaxing piece of pie.

The song was one of ten that Cobain, Novoselic and Crover recorded on January 23, 1988, at Jack Endino's Reciprocal Studios in Seattle. The recordings were meant to be used as a demo tape, but 'Floyd the Barber' received airplay on Seattle radio station KCMU, and in fact the version that appears on *Bleach* is simply a remix of the Crover demo. (The band attempted to record the song again, with Chad Channing on drums, but remained happier with the Crover version.)

Ironically, and somewhat chillingly, *The Andy Griffith Show* may have been one of the last things that Kurt Cobain saw in this world – it was broadcast on the station he had his home television tuned to on the day he took his life.

about a girl

among all the dark, churning riffs and proto-grunge thunder of *Bleach*, one song beamed out as a stunning shot of pop sunlight (albeit some uncommonly sad pop sunlight) – the hook-built, Beatle-crafted 'About a Girl'. The song also stands out in the Cobain canon as a song with a very specific genesis and a very real subject.

The girl in question was Cobain's girlfriend at the time, Tracy Marander, and the song was written when she asked Kurt if he might not have anything to say about her or their relationship in a song. At one point, Cobain might have put some sweeter sentiments into the song, but by the time he wrote 'About a Girl', he and Marander were pulling apart. The result is a small pop gem, perfectly capturing the rage, hurt and residual tenderness of a fractured, failing romance and packing it all into verses and choruses that are unstoppably catchy.

Cobain met Marander through his punk mentor – Buzz Osborne of the Melvins. Beginning at the end of 1986, Cobain was spending more and more time in Olympia. Students at Evergreen College in Olympia supported a small but fervent underground music scene, in which the Melvins were big fish. Marander was a Melvins acquaintance with dyed-red hair who was taken with the blonde, blue-eyed boy responsible for both the jagged art-punk on the Fecal Matter cassette (Fecal Matter were Cobain's first band) and the accomplished image of KISS painted on the side of the Melvin's gig-to-gig vehicle, better known as the Mel-van. Kurt, in turn, was smitten, and was soon spending weekends at Tracy's apartment at 114 North Pear Street in Olympia. In September 1987 he left his own apartment on East 2nd Street in Aberdeen altogether and moved in with Marander.

The two had some undeniably deep feelings for each other, but it wasn't too long before the atmosphere at North Pear Street grew troubled.

Sweet melodies often turned ferocious at Nirvana gigs.

Cobain wasn't always in flannel, wasn't always bashing out heavy riffs, and wasn't always listening to dark, angry punks. He greatly enjoyed the pop craftsman-ship of the Smithereens, and used their sound as an inspiration when he wrote 'About a Girl.'

Marander was devotedly supportive of Kurt's musical ambitions and shared some of his tastes in found art and home decoration – the two of them turned the place into a rather untidy gallery of home-made sculptures and installations. But Cobain's feelings towards domestic responsibilities – particularly rent-paying – weren't always easy for Marander to put up with. He sometimes responded to her entreaties to find employment by casually offering to move out and live in his car. He summed up the situation with the song's line "I can't see you every night for free".

Musically, the song seems to have grown from some of Cobain's more mainstream pop influences. "I hear the Smithereens' 'Blood and Roses' as a direct precursor to 'About a Girl'," says Jon Auer of the Posies, a Seattle scene contemporary of Nirvana's, known for their pop rather than "grunge" approach to song writing. "The Posies shared a soundman with Nirvana for a while, so I know for a fact that Kurt was way into the Smithereens.

And if you check it out you hear the similarities – the simple, repetitive structures that are really cool. That's what Kurt got into."

Marander and Cobain's on-again/off-again relationship was tested again after Bleach was released and Nirvana began to tour – Kurt might send her loving postcards from the road, but when they were together times were tense.

Marander finally moved out of the North Pear Street house in June of 1990, and Cobain continued to live there, taking in Dave Grohl as a roommate when the drummer joined the band in September. Later, Cobain and Marander had a brief period of reconciliation just prior to the release of Nevermind.

In addition to 'About a Girl', Marander is responsible for one other prominent piece of the Nirvana story – she took the photo that became the cover shot for Bleach.

school

Of all the festering complaints and settling of scores that the songs on *Bleach* give voice to, 'School' is the one that most powerfully makes its point with the scantiest of lyrics. No story is told, no indictment read – the meaning is made clear through the singer's repeated cries of "No recess." It's the angry but unsurprised yell of someone who's been ripped off, but who expects no less from the powers that be – the cry of someone who takes an almost masochistic satisfaction in the fact that the one little bearable piece of a nearly unbearable situation has been, predictably, snatched away.

Although 'School' undoubtedly exorcized some lingering high school demons, the song was actually written about Seattle and, to some extent, about Sub Pop. For a while these inspirations were made explicitly clear in the song's working title – 'The Seattle Scene.' Cobain's complaint was that, having escaped the soul-sapping confines of Aberdeen for the supposed freedoms of Seattle, he perceived the same kind of cliquishness, snobbery and social politics among the city's music-scene makers that had made high school such a nightmare for him. All that work to escape and here he was, for all intents and purposes, stuck in school again.

By most accounts, actual school-time was never enjoyable for Kurt. Typical junior high school report card comments tagged him as a "restless, bored and uncooperative" student. At Aberdeen High School, Cobain made a half-hearted go of it for a while, barely getting by as he spent his days in class either slumbering or eyeing instructors with murderous contempt. His one refuge was in art classes, where he could occasionally put some of his talents to enjoyable use. By eleventh grade, time at school was spent mainly at a smokers' shed in the school grounds. During senior year, with his class's graduation looming in the not-to-distant future, Cobain considered applying himself to a schedule of remedial courses in order to catch up. But with nearly two years of courses to make up in less than six months, Cobain called it quits. He wasn't a part of his high school class when it graduated in June of 1985 – he had dropped out a few weeks before.

Socially, Cobain didn't fare much better than he did scholastically. He had sensed early on in his schoolyard life that it was not going to be easy for him to "get along well with others." He felt like a misfit, and was frequently treated like one by shifting squads of bullies and jocks. Not that Cobain had very much desire to fit in with the prevailing cliques at Aberdeen High. Clearly he wanted no part of the jock crowd, but his other options seemed pretty much limited to groups of hopelessly uninformed nerds and hopelessly disengaged stoners. Cobain drifted through both groups without making any strong connections or friendships.

It was at the smokers' shed where at least one important friendship finally did begin to take shape – with a punk-rock loving drummer named Dale Crover, who had recently begun playing with the Melvins. Melvins rehearsals became the one place where Cobain not only felt accepted, but also saw a social group he wanted to be a part of. Guitarist Osborne, bassist Matt Lukin – a longtime Cobain acquaintance – and drummer Crover responded by taking Cobain under their wing and giving him a "punk" education. At Aberdeen High, Kurt was also aware of one other person who looked like he might be somebody worth knowing – a gangly goofball named Krist Novoselic. But their friendship would not begin in earnest until school was just an unpleasant memory to be kicked about in a howling tune.

bleach

Life after Aberdeen wasn't without its bummers. Cobain decried the arty egos and cliquishness of Seattle's music scene by comparing it to one of his least favorite places: School.

In the Sub Pop family with tourmates TAD. Back row: Everman, Doyle, Novoselic, Cobain and Channing.

this cover tune became an unlikely but effective calling card for Nirvana when it became the A-side of their first Sub Pop single in November 1988 – the first in Sub Pop's "Single of the Month" releases.

The song became a highlight of the band's shows, even before the band became Nirvana. In the winter of 1987, Kurt, Krist and drummer Aaron Burckhard were a nameless trio working on a short set's worth of art-noise originals (some of which had survived from the Fecal Matter days) and covers of favorites such as Flipper's 'Sex Bomb'. Kurt and Krist had complementary musical tastes – both had done a fair amount of hanging out to the over-sized rock of Black Sabbath and Led Zeppelin, and both had undergone the "Melvinization" process of Aberdeen punk godfather Buzz Osborne that led them toward the Sex Pistols, Flipper and the Butthole Surfers. But Krist also had an interest in the occasional treasures to be found among the older, obscure albums piled into bargain bins at record stores.

He was particularly excited by the music he discovered when he got his hands on an out-of-print album by the Dutch band Shocking Blue – whose main claim to fame had been the 1970 chart-topper 'Venus'. The bassist promptly turned his fledgling band-partner on to the newly discovered oddity, and though Kurt wasn't as charmed by the band's subdued psychedelia as Krist was, he agreed to work up a version of one of the record's headiest pop tunes, 'Love Buzz'. When the still-nameless trio played its first party gigs, 'Love Buzz' was on the set list, and when, under the moniker Skid Row, the band played its first proper gigs at the GESSCO Hall in Olympia and the Community World Theater in Tacoma, the song earned the band some of its heartiest responses.

The Jack Endino-recorded demo tape of January 1988 (with the Melvins' Dale Crover on drums) had aroused the interest of Sub Pop's Jonathan Poneman. But he was even more impressed with the over-the-top cover of 'Love Buzz' he witnessed at several early band

love buzz

performances. When he asked the group to do a single for the label, he suggested the song. Kurt and Krist liked the idea of recording something new, rather than re-recording a track from the demo, and though Kurt pushed for an original, he eventually conceded that 'Love Buzz' had a good mix of edge and accessibility. The main session for the single was done on June 11, 1988, with Endino behind the recording console at the Reciprocal studio in Seattle, just a few weeks after Chad Channing had begun drumming with the group. On the original 7-inch release, the song begins with a 10-second sound collage of cooing voices from a children's record that Cobain had been entertained by. The collage was pulled when *Bleach* was assembled.

'Love Buzz' was written by Robbie van Leeuwen, guitarist for Shocking Blue. The group came together in 1967, and also included bassist Klassje van der Wal, drummer Cor van Beek, and vocalist Fred de Wilde. After they released one single, de Wilde was replaced by the alluring Mariska Veres, who had previously sung with a group called the Bumble Bees. The group reached the pinnacle of its success in February of 1970, when 'Venus' spent a week at number 1 on the American pop charts. The band had some further chart climbers in the early 1970s with tracks such as 'Hello Darkness,' 'Shocking You' and 'Blossom Lady,' but major success eluded them and the band broke up in 1974.

Nirvana were actually the second band of the 1980s to enjoy some good fortune with a song by Shocking Blue – Bananarama's cover of 'Venus' went to number 1 on the American charts for a week in September 1986.

Shocking Blue in prime 'Venus' and 'Love Buzz' form, circa 1969.

paper cuts

a long with 'Floyd the Barber,' 'Paper Cuts' was one of the two tracks from the demo that the band recorded with Dale Crover on drums in January 1988 to make it on to *Bleach*. (A third, 'Downer' was not included on the original vinyl pressing of *Bleach* but was included on the CD version of the album.)

From the time he dropped out of school in spring 1985, and

A post-*Bleach* photo session finds future Nirvana drummer Dave Grohl.

throughout most of 1986, Cobain had no fixed place to stay. There were occasional nights spent at his mother's house, but he was more comfortable crashing at friends' homes. Novoselic or Crover put him up frequently, but Cobain also spent a fair number of nights outdoors, sleeping under the North Aberdeen Bridge. Eventually he moved into the home of some friends, Steve and Eric Shillinger, whose father was an English teacher at Aberdeen High.

During this aimless period, the mostly unemployed Kurt began spending time with a local small-time drug-dealer. The dealer figures in the Cobain story chiefly for getting Kurt briefly hooked on painkillers that the dealer had been stealing from pharmacies in the area, and for giving Cobain his first shot of heroin. The dealer was often in the company of a tag-along, damaged-goods sidekick – who seemed utterly devoted to the dealer despite the harsh treatment he often received. The story of this sad hanger-on's background became the basis for 'Paper Cuts'.

Home as hell: Cobain came up with his screaming indictments in 'Paper Cuts' after hearing a true, horrific story of some abused children imprisoned in their parents' house.

The kid had come from a home in Aberdeen where the abusive parents had kept several children constantly locked in a single room. The windows were painted over with black paint and the only concession to hygiene was a pile of newspapers that the kids were expected to use as their toilet. Just enough food was thrown into the room to give the children basic sustenance. When this atrocious situation was discovered by the authorities, the children were taken away and the parents prosecuted. The story understandably created quite a stir in Aberdeen.

'Paper Cuts' is written from the point of view of one of those trapped, terrified, confused children. Cobain describes the food being pushed through the door, the darkened windows and the filth in a voice that ranges from eerily gentle sing-song to crazed shriek. But pulling away from the facts of the case, Cobain also wrote some lines about the entrapped subject's relationship with his mother – a relationship that may have also been partly based on his own conflicted relationship with his mother, Wendy. He describes looking at her with "maternal love," but is pained that she cannot bear to look him in the eyes.

The song is also notable in that it makes use of the word that Cobain and Novoselic would finally settle on as their band name – and the "nirvana" described in 'Paper Cuts' makes obvious Cobain's ironic intentions. The subject seems to sing that he has found his "nirvana" and is in a contented state in a place where all needs are met and there are no outside worries. But to any outside observer, the subject has simply gone insane in a filthy, one-room prison.

'Negative Creep' – a witty, scathing autobiography.

though much of the anger packed into the songs on *Bleach* was aimed at figures of authority or control, Cobain never positions himself as a righteous rebel or fighter of the good fight. As someone who'd grown up racked with self-doubts, he wasn't about to take on the persona of a super-confident speaker of punk truths in his songs (the way that Joe Strummer, Johnny Rotten or even Iggy Pop had). The voice Cobain developed in his song writing rarely spoke from any position of power, unless that power was used in a display of self-loathing – which is what's heard in a song such as 'Negative Creep.' Listeners got a fairly open, darkly humorous self-assessment from the songwriter – pretty much summed up by the song's title.

The other point Cobain chose to make in this tune – not only does he identify himself as a negative creep, he also lets us know he's "stoned" – was certainly no stretch of the songwriter's imagination. Life in Aberdeen didn't offer Cobain a great deal of mental stimulation, and so as a teenager he sought out the adventuresome highs and numbing comforts of a variety of drugs. By the time Cobain wrote 'Negative Creep', he was a regular pot smoker, had extensive experience with hallucinogens, had already kicked a Percodan habit and had tried heroin.

negative creep

scoff

Musically, the song represents one of the "Sub Pop-iest" of Nirvana tracks – it's a true "grunge" track, with barely a glimmer of that pop craft that Cobain was coming to be capable of. The song's dark, churning bass and guitar riff creates a semi-industrial assault that never lets up, and Cobain's vocals are for the most part a single yelped note of confession. 'Negative Creep' gets its point across effectively, but doesn't seem quite as deep as tunes such as 'School' or 'Blew', in which the tension and release in Cobain's voice shape some similarly ugly sentiments. The track sounds like it might be equally at home on a Mudhoney album and, in fact, the band did get some guff from some in the Seattle scene for using the line "Daddy's little girl ain't a girl no more," which was uncomfortably similar to Mudhoney's "Sweet Young Thing Ain't Sweet No More."

Cobain sometimes mocked himself for what he saw as his limitations as a song writer – his reliance on the verse-chorus-verse structure and a handful of ear-grabbing tricks. But, when he was feeling more charitable toward his talents, he demonstrated a great deal of pride in his ability to write well-built tunes with unstoppable hooks. One of the instrumental hooks of 'Negative Creep' – one of its best "tricks" – comes from the sudden rhythmic stops in the verses, which are filled by a squirrelly guitar note and a throaty Cobain cry. He would use the same kind of stops, guitar notes and cries at the end of the chorus of the band's biggest single, 'Smells Like Teen Spirit'.

In a few short years, after *Nevermind* had sold several million copies, Cobain would bristle when hearing himself referred to as "the voice of a generation." But at the point when he was writing songs for *Bleach* he still had plenty of fresh memories of encounters with those who did not consider him to be a voice worth hearing at all. 'Scoff' is Cobain's angrily concise response to those who might have offered encouragement to him but who "scoffed" instead. As writer Michael Azerrad has pointed out, it's quite possible that the song was most directly targeted at Cobain's parents – a kind of final blast of recrimination before Cobain and the band moved physically, economically and psychologically far from Aberdeen.

The song is one of *Bleach*'s more confrontational tracks. The singer is aware of how he is seen by the targets of the song – as a problem child who's "not worth" the trouble he causes. But Cobain, with some rare un-ironic self-confidence, lets it be known that he doesn't consider himself lazy and insists that his life story isn't over, despite the dim expectations others have for him. His response to the lack of support he's received is to demand his alcohol. Presumably, if his parents – or parental figures of some sort – have already written him off, they don't have much right to withhold something that does offer some comfort.

Happy and as yet uncomplicated: the days between *Bleach* and *Nevermind*.

swap meet

eager bargain-hunters.

While some might view the swap meet as an indication of small town community values, Cobain saw instead a sad and ugly spectacle in which people of little means tried to get by, selling off their junk to people of similarly reduced means.

A particularly odd product of the swap meets, in Cobain's eyes, was the creation of an underclass of "professional" swap-meeters, who would travel from town to town to hawk whatever nearly worthless goods they had to offer. Those are the kind of folk he had in mind when creating the characters who drift from meet to meet and meal to meal in the song.

The "he" and "she" of the song are clearly distasteful characters to Cobain, but the song doesn't come across solely as a snicker at their expense. The singer seems not to be without some sympathy for these pathetic souls when describing their hard lives, especially when he takes time to tell us that each of them keeps some cherished possessions close to their hearts – for him it's cigarettes, for her it's photographs, and for both of them it's a lump of unrelenting bitterness.

The standard arts and crafts fare of the swap meet was captured in the song with a reference to bric-a-brac knocked together out of seashells, driftwood and burlap.

This kind of handicraft was used again by the band to more humorous effect in their first press biography for Geffen Records, which was released with *Nevermind*. In the biography, Cobain is described as a "sawblade painter" who specializes in wildlife and landscapes, and is said to have met Novoselic at "the Grays Harbor Institute of Northwest Crafts."

Novoselic is described as the one with the passion for "gluing seashells and driftwood on burlap" and, in describing how he developed an artistic chemistry with Cobain, is quoted as saying:

"I liked what Kurt was doing. I asked him what his thoughts were on a macaroni mobile I was working on. He suggested I glue glitter on it. That really made it!"

Life in the slow lane – Nirvana eats up (with post-*Bleach* drummer Dan Peters, in cap). The biggest local attraction in Aberdeen, swap meets, became a running joke between Cobain and Novoselic. Cobain turned two sad vendors into the subjects of 'Swap Meet.'

While, in 'Floyd the Barber', Cobain gleefully sketched out some smalltown characters whose small minds contained murderous impulses, the pair of small-towners he depicted in 'Swap Meet' were hardly a threat. The song takes a harsh look at a couple of unremarkable losers – a man and woman who are eking out a gray living as junk-sellers, unable ever to express the feelings they have for each other.

The song took its name from a kind of grass-roots entrepreneurship that Cobain witnessed often in Aberdeen. The swap meet – like the flea market or yard sale – was a way for individuals to make a little money by selling cast-offs, knick-knacks, home-made foods, arts and crafts and unwanted miscellany to

Beware furry faces; for Cobain the symbol of dumb, swaggering machismo.

mr. moustache

speaker's identity obvious or telling much of a story.

What is clear is that, to Cobain, the moustache was a symbol of the kind of brain-deadened machismo he'd come to hate in schoolmates and townfolks. This hate wasn't born merely of principle – Cobain had suffered several schoolyard beatings at the hands of the jock element in his school because he was presumed to be a "faggot." At one point he took to answering gay-baiting taunts by insisting that he was, in fact, gay – and almost hoped that the claim proved true, as it would mean he was truly different from those he despised. But he was not, and eventually simply avoided as best he could the Mr. Moustaches of his school.

Cobain's vision of Mr. Moustache was made explicit in a cartoon he inked into a notebook at about the same time he wrote the song. Mr. Moustache lives in an

mr. Moustache isn't described in the song that bears his name – he is either speaking the lyrics or is on the receiving end of them. It isn't clear, or perhaps even important, whether Cobain, posing as a typical Mr. Moustache, is sneeringly asking some addle-brained hippie types for enlightenment, or whether Cobain is sarcastically asking some moustachioed macho man for tips on more manly living. The ripping, metallic riffs and the impressionistic punches of lyrics about beef-eating ("Yes, I eat cow"), constipation ("Poop as hard as rock") and ill will ("I don't like you anyway") set the mood of menace and mistrust without making the

Riding redneck: Steve Abini's 'Big Black' screamed out against moustaches and the state of Texas in a song named after that state. Cobain picked up the anti-macho, anti-facial hair scream with 'Mr. Moustache'.

apartment where a gun, a mounted animal head and a large collection of hunting caps decorate the walls. With an open beer in one hand, he listens in to the sounds emanating from his pregnant wife's belly and surmises that the fetus has strong enough legs to become a powerful football player. He launches into a rant about how the child had better not turn out to be a girl – he's got his hopes set on an "honest, hard workin', Jew-, spic-, nigger-, and faggot-hatin', 100%-pure-beef American male." Mr. Moustache also looks forward to teaching his son how to work on cars and exploit women. With his rage exhausted for a moment, Mr. Moustache again rests his head against wife's belly. In the final frame of the cartoon, the powerful little fetal leg that Mr. Moustache had such high hopes for comes smashing through Momma's belly and – with plenty of attendant gore – drives right through good ol' Dad's friggin' face.

It's possible that Cobain's anti-moustache stance may have been influenced by the work of future *In Utero* producer Steve Albini, whose influential, Chicago-based

guitar-thrash unit, Big Black, played a pivotal, scene-uniting show in March 1987 at the Showbox in Seattle. In one of Big Black's more rousing, anti-macho attacks, 'Texas', the singer proclaimed, "I hate moustache."

Cobain's anti-authoritarian messages were prominent not only in songs.

VANDALISM: BEAUTIFUL AS A ROCK IN A COP'S FACE

sifting

the lyrics for 'Sifting' were pulled together as the *Bleach* sessions were commencing and, with Cobain tired, stressed and not at the top of his word-game, were not intended to convey a great deal of meaning. But, as was usually the case with Cobain, he managed to find a few words that carried power beyond their specific references. At its most heated, the song is an effective kiss-off to the kind of authority figures who had been of little use or help to Cobain – teachers and preachers. In 'Sifting', these characters seem to look deep into the singer's eyes, and then admit that they have nothing to offer him. The emphasis on "eyes" may have come from some real encounters with these types – if teachers remembered nothing else about Cobain as a kid, they tended to remember his blazing blue eyes.

The rest of the song doesn't offer much in the way of a coherent message, but it does demonstrate what would become a trademark of Cobain's lyrics – his sense of playfulness with words. In school settings Cobain was never a top student, but he was a voracious reader on his own terms. He had a simple love for the sheer pleasure of rhyme – "Cross says floss" and "Search for church" have a Dr. Seuss quality in their simplicity. Furthermore, while Cobain was obviously more concerned with getting a punk band off the ground than in indulging in literary experiments, he had already become a devoted reader of such "underground" authors as William Burroughs and Charles Bukowski ("Bukowski, Beckett, anyone with a 'B'", he joked of his reading tastes). Burroughs's work, in particular, may have opened Cobain's mind to the idea that simple words and phrases could become fascinating when used unconventionally. Cobain took a step towards bending language to suit his own whims with 'Sifting.'

Cobain's politics were never made explicit in his lyrics – he didn't write protest songs. But in works like 'Sifting' he presented himself as an angry victim of a variety of authority figures.

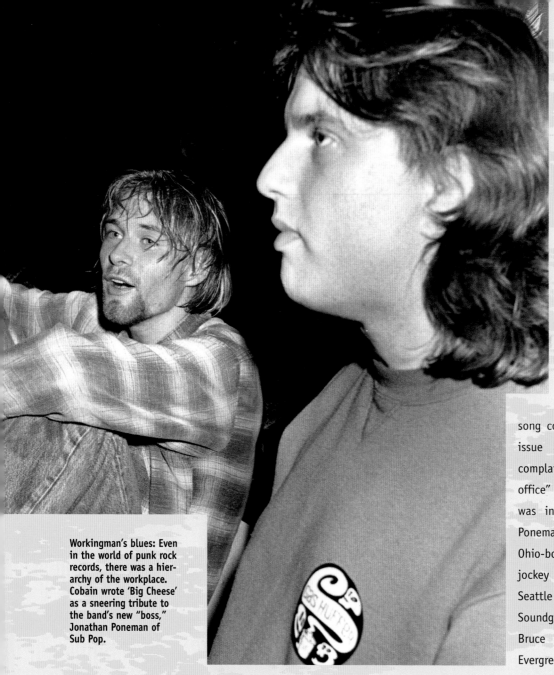

Workingman's blues: Even in the world of punk rock records, there was a hierarchy of the workplace. Cobain wrote 'Big Cheese' as a sneering tribute to the band's new "boss," Jonathan Poneman of Sub Pop.

big cheese

this song was originally released as the B-side to the 'Love Buzz' single in November 1988. It had been recorded by Jack Endino in the same June 11, 1988, session that yielded 'Love Buzz', a song called 'Blandest' and a second version of 'Spank Thru', which would later appear on the seminal *Sup Pop 200* collection. While the song comes across as a kind of standard-issue anti-authority rant, with Cobain complaining about being sent to "the office" by the titular cheese, that cheese was in fact a real person – Jonathan Poneman of Sub Pop records.

Ohio-born Poneman was working as a disc jockey and a promoter of local shows in Seattle when he was introduced, by Soundgarden-guitarist Kim Thayil, to one Bruce Pavitt, a one-time student at Evergreen State College in Olympia and self-made publisher of an underground music fanzine entitled *Sub Pop*. The two hit it off, decided to team their talents behind a small record label Pavitt had just begun, and were soon putting out such seminal "Seattle Sound" recordings as Soundgarden's 1988 'Screaming Life' EP on the Sub Pop record label.

Pavitt and Poneman envisioned a label that would have an identifiable Northwest look, sound and style – somewhat akin to the way Berry Gordy had organized and directed the artists on the Motown label in Detroit, or the way that the Stax label had perfectly captured the mid-60's musical vibe of Memphis. The pair heard a fresh, regional sound in the jolting mix of punk energy and metal bombast offered by Seattle bands such as Green River (members of which would go on to form Pearl Jam and Mudhoney). And the music came with a natural, home-grown look and spirit – the flannel-shirted, work-booted populism of disaffected, working class kids. In its grainy, unglamorous band photos, self-deprecating press releases and in its fierce, guitar-driven music, Sub Pop indeed began to capture and redefine the image of the Seattle music scene.

Poneman was always on the lookout for new, exciting bands that he could bring into the Sub Pop fold, and rumor of a trio of unschooled, un-pretty kids from Aberdeen who were capable of pop hooks and metallic roar naturally caught his interest. He loved the music they made as soon as he heard it – Jack Endino passed a copy of the demo that Kurt and Krist had recorded with Dale Crover in January at Reciprocal, and Poneman was taken with the power of tracks such as 'Floyd the Barber' and 'Downer'. Poneman and Pavitt both had day jobs at Muzak – the music corporation responsible for most of the tinkling, neutered versions of pop songs played in elevators and grocery stores – and Poneman brought the tape in to play for his partner. Pavitt wasn't so enthusiastic, but Poneman stayed interested enough to set up a meeting with Cobain and Novoselic at the Cafe Roma coffeehouse on Broadway in Seattle. Despite Kurt's lack of desire to talk much, and Krist's drunkenness, Poneman managed to get them interested in recording a single for Sub Pop.

Cobain and Novoselic were in fact quite excited about actually recording their songs and getting a single out, but Cobain quickly realized that even in the free-thinking world of underground music, there were bosses who needed to be answered to. While the band had been continuing to explore some noisy, art-punk, Melvins-ish song structures, the Sub Pop sound that Poneman and Pavitt wanted to push forward was a more stream-lined rock n' roll sound, built on straight-ahead rhythms and driving guitar. So, almost immediately, Cobain was taking direction from a record label, and rather than having his first single be a weirder, personal favorite like 'Hairspray Queen', he was convinced by Poneman to go with the catchier – and more marketable – 'Love Buzz'. Cobain

was rankled enough – and amused enough – to work out the mix of gratitude and resentment he felt toward Poneman in a song.

'Blandest' was intended to be the 'Love Buzz' B-side, but at the insistence of Endino, the band and Poneman agreed to go with the more striking 'Big Cheese' instead. After the initial June recording session, the song was punched up in a second session, and was mixed in mid-July. But, in true big-cheese fashion, Poneman made it clear that he wasn't happy with the vocals, and asked Cobain to re-record them. The re-recorded version is what Sub Pop released in November.

"I was expressing all the pressures that I felt from him at the time because he was being so judgmental about what we were recording," Cobain told Michael Azerrad in *Come As You Are*.

Before recording with Sub Pop, Cobain knew the label through its release of a favorite record – Soungarden's 1988 'Screaming Life' EP. Nirvana recorded with Jack Endino at Reciprocal Recording because they liked the sound Soundgarden had gotten there.

As 'Downer' indicates, getting stoned didn't stop Cobain from feeling glum.

'**d**owner' was included on *Bleach* when the album – originally only available on vinyl – was re-released on CD after the wild success of *Nevermind*. The same track also turned up as one of the collection of demos, rarities and B-sides featured on *Incesticide*.

Lyrically, the song is a fairly typical growled-out hunk of Cobain dismay, but musically it's repetitive, jackhammer beat and the leap from softly-spoken verses to yelled choruses sounds less like a presage of Nirvana tunes to come and more like a track inspired by the mid-80s Chicago sound of Steve Albini's Big Black. 'Downer' also stands out among the Bleach tracks as being the song with the longest history.

Cobain had become friendly with a classmate in Aberdeen who also spent a good deal of time at the high school smokers' shed – Dale Crover. Crover was recognized as one of the better drummers in the area, and had jammed with most of the guitarists in town, including Krist Novoselic's brother, Robert. Krist told Buzz Osborne about Crover when Osborne was looking for a hard-hitting drummer who could play with punk speed, and Crover soon not only became a Melvin but turned a room at his parents' house into the Melvins' rehearsal space. One of those who began dropping in regularly to check out the

downer

rehearsals was Crover's friend, Cobain.

Cobain auditioned for the Melvins in Spring 1984, but choked under pressure and failed to impress anybody with his guitar skills. He instead began concentrating on his own songs, and by the end of 1985 felt that he had a bunch worth recording. His mother's sister, Mary Fradenburg, was a guitarist who owned a four-track recorder and so Cobain rounded up Crover to play bass, brought in a friend named Greg Hokanson to play drums, and began fronting his first band – unpromisingly named Fecal Matter. They recorded seven songs, which were built mainly on loud, fast, semi-metallic riffs and punk yells – Cobain wasn't yet tapping his talent for powerfully catchy melodies. One of the slower tunes that Fecal Matter recorded would live longer than that particular line-up – it was a heavy instrumental track entitled 'Downer.'

The cassette of Fecal Matter songs was to bring Cobain together with Krist Novoselic. Cobain made a point of hounding the bassist, and frequently suggested that they should try getting a band together, but for a while Novoselic didn't seem particularly interested. Finally, when Krist made a point of listening to what was on the tape, he thought he heard something worth pursuing and quickly let Cobain know that, yes indeed, they should start making some music together.

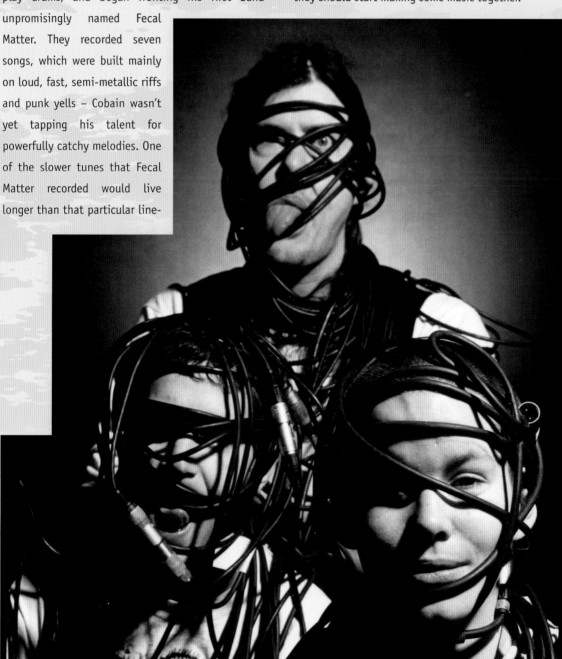

The ugly churn of 'Downer' didn't hit the popcraft to come from Cobain. It was one of the first songs he ever wrote, and was rooted in the edgier approach of such early Cobain-heroes as Austin, Texas-based psycho-noisemakers the Butthole Surfers.

nevermind

Notes from the underground packed into a beautiful clamor – Nirvana's masterwork was a revolutionary blend of pop, punk rage, art and rock n' roll.

irvana followed up the modest *sturm und drang* of *Bleach* with the most radical action a punk-inspired band could take – they created a pop masterpiece, sold millions of records and changed the course of rock n' roll. Not bad for a band from Aberdeen.

Nevermind harnessed all the grungy, punky power the band had aspired to, and were capable of – the bass parts throbbed, the guitars roared and the drum parts rumbled with almost super-human thunder. But what immediately jumped out of *Nevermind*, and resolutely grabbed hold of the listener's head, was the songs. These were, beyond the distortion units and haggardly screamed vocals, perfectly crafted, quintessentially catchy pop-tune constructions. Cobain's songs satisfied all the guilty pleasures of hook-filled Top-40 tracks of the 1970s, but what was there for any listener to feel guilty about? These songs weren't built-for-market confections. They raged with honest intensity and shined a light into the ugly psychic corners of the song writer and the audience.

The amazing thing was, the audience sang along.

Nevermind, like most other ground-shaking rock albums before it, was both a work of forward vision and sturdy tradition. *Sgt Pepper* succeeded as a work of cutting-edge, artsy ambition, but its music consistently harkened back to the broad entertainment values of the music hall. *Never Mind the Bollocks Here's the Sex Pistols* rang out as punk's most anarchic salvo, but on closer inspection what made the record great, and what has made it last, was that the Pistols simply wrote great, unabashed rock n' roll songs – as much a product of Chuck Berry as the London scene of 1976. Similarly, while *Nevermind* undoubtedly swept up its listeners with an energy that was daring and fresh, the songs themselves were simply wonderfully executed lessons in popcraft – the same kind of popcraft that worked for such pop masters as the Raspberries, the Turtles or Cheap Trick.

Cobain himself would frequently point out that he didn't consider himself to be the first song writer to pump up punk noise with a heart of pop – he cited the Pixies's *Surfer Rosa* as an album that had a particular influence on his writing for *Nevermind*; and also paid due tribute to acts such as Hüsker Dü and the Meat Puppets. But, to give Cobain his due, never before had such extremes been so brilliantly combined. Never before had a band been able to be simultaneously as loud and as light, as pop and as punk, as Nirvana. The humble band from Aberdeen had produced a thoroughly compelling work – *Nevermind*'s sweet screams vented deep alienation at the same time as they offered an irresistible invitation. The underground was startled; the mainstream was rapt; and the rules of the rock n' roll marketplace changed overnight. Michael Jackson was out, Nirvana was in.

But before Nirvana could turn the pop world upside down, there were several changes that took place in their own sphere. The band had been continually developing strength as a live act and had received several rave reviews from their first trip to the East Coast – in 1989 – but it became increasingly obvious that the more conventionally rock-oriented Jason Everman was not happy as a member of the band. After a show at the Pyramid Club in New York – as part of that year's New Music Seminar – the band canceled some Midwestern dates and drove home, barely speaking to each other. Everman became an ex-member of Nirvana. (He went on to play bass briefly with Soundgarden, played with New Jersey-based Mindfunk and then joined the U.S. Navy.)

As a trio again, the band began to think about recording a second album for Sub Pop, and began work on new songs. In April 1990, with the working title *Sheep* in mind, the band went to Smart Studios in Madison, Wisconsin, to record some demos with producer Butch Vig, who had some strong underground

music credentials – Killdozer, Laughing Hyenas, Smashing Pumpkins – and who had done excellent work with the *8 Way Santa* album from Nirvana tourmates and label-mates, TAD. They recorded seven songs with Vig, five of which turned up on *Nevermind* (including a version of 'Polly' that was simply remixed for the album).

After accompanying the band on its first European tour, and contributing to the Smart demos and sessions for that summer's 'Blew' EP, Chad Channing was gently dismissed from the group. Novoselic and Cobain still felt kindly toward Channing, but had become dissatisfied with his abilities as a drummer. The band played again briefly with Dale Crover. Then Mudhoney-drummer Dan Peters was brought in for one gig – he played on the 'Sliver'/'Dive' single that was released in 1990 – but he soon returned to his own band.

Finally, it was Nirvana-Samaritan Buzz Osborne who came to the drumming rescue – by setting up a meeting between Kurt, Krist and Dave Grohl, a young drummer

Getting a grip – with drummer Dave Grohl, Nirvana got the big sound they'd always wanted.

from a Washington D.C. hardcore band called Scream. He was exactly the kind of sharp, musical, tremendously hard-hitting drummer they'd always wanted to work with – and the chemistry was right. Grohl was in, and the Nirvana of *Nevermind* and beyond was set to roll.

While Nirvana remained appreciative of the initial breaks they had received from Bruce Pavitt and Jonathan Poneman of Sub Pop, they were growing frustrated with the fact that the label's lack of resources was making it hard for them to get their music to the public. Distribution was poor – *Bleach* was still hard to find; and the label could offer only minimal support while the band was on tour. When, in 1990, some of Sub Pop's overly ambitious distribution deals began to fail, the band decided that – punk credibility notwithstanding – they could shop around for a decent deal from a major label.

Using the Smart Studios demos as a teaser, the band and, somewhat inadvertently, Sub Pop had managed to create a considerable Nirvana buzz among major labels. Throughout the winter of 1990-91, the scruffy trio were wined and dined by various A&R men and label honchos. In April 1991, the band decided to follow the example of punk-heroes (and Nirvana boosters) Sonic Youth by signing with Geffen records.

Through May and June 1991, the band worked at Sound City studios, located just north of Los Angeles in suburban Van Nuys, California. The band put in a lot of 10- and 12-hour days over six weeks, working again with Vig. When tracks were finished, they were mixed by Andy Wallace, who was a hot name at the time thanks to his work on Slayer's album *Seasons in the Abyss*. Though Vig himself helped encourage Cobain to embrace a kind of subversive pop approach in his writing and in-studio performances, it was Wallace's mixes that gave the tunes a definitive pop sheen.

During those sessions, Cobain became re-acquainted with a woman who would come to play a large role in his life – Courtney Love. He had met her previously at a Nirvana show in Portland, and met her again through her connections with Dave Grohl – she was a friend of L7-bassist Jennifer Finch, who was an ex-girlfriend of Grohl's. Romance did not blossom immediately, but Cobain and Love both acknowledged the stirrings of some deep feelings between them.

It seems almost comical now that when Geffen Records first released *Nevermind*, in September of 1991, it was with a pressing of less than 50,000 records. A month later, the record debuted on the Billboard charts at number 144. The band continued to tour non-stop and soon radio and MTV had picked up on the album's single, 'Smells Like Teen Spirit'. By the first week of November, the album was in the Top 40. Weeks later it cracked the Top 10, and by Christmas of that year almost 400,000 copies a week of *Nevermind* were being sold. Nirvana took Michael Jackson's place and became the owners of the number one album spot on the U.S. pop charts.

Those who bought *Nevermind* not only got a full dose of Nirvana, they also got a good look at five-month-old Spencer Elden, the submerged, naked infant swimming after a hooked dollar bill on *Nevermind*'s now famous cover. (Despite some record company nervousness, the

band insisted that Spencer's penis not be airbrushed away.) The CD booklet included some randomly selected lines of *Nevermind* lyrics cut together into a poem. The credits listed the bass player as Chris Novoselic – he would not reclaim his given name of Krist until 1993's *In Utero*. But the band's guitarist, vocalist and song writer, returned to the spelling of his name as it appeared on his birth certificate. The fellow listed as Kurdt Kobain on *Bleach*, was now known as Kurt Cobain.

Unlike the infant on their album's cover, Nirvana kept their pants on for the first *Nevermind* publicity photos.

nevermind's phenomenal first single (backed with 'Drain You') was released just prior to the album, in August 1991. The song was the perfect archetype of the Nirvana sound and the Cobain song. It had amazing lurches in dynamics, moving back and forth between gentle strums and monstrous thrashing. It also had a remarkably catchy melody that sounded both sunny and sad, and it was full of lyrics that nobody could make any sense out of.

While the songs on *Nevermind* wouldn't offer much more explicit, easily grasped meaning than those of

Bleach, Cobain's lyrics were now one with his voice – his despondency, wrath, rage, disgust and humor all came through perfectly clearly, no matter how inscrutable his actual words were.

As it turned out, while *Nevermind*'s most popular track was a typically murky Cobain exploration of meaning and meaninglessness, it had come to him by way of a very specific inspiration – namely, a deodorant. While Cobain was living on North Pear Street in Olympia, he had gone out one night with his friend Kathleen Hanna from the band Bikini Kill, a group that would become a pivotal force in the punk-feminist "Riot Grrl" movement of Olympia and Seattle. They decided to

indulge one of their frequent recreational bents – a graffiti spree. After marking up some Olympia establishments with such incitements as "God is Gay," they returned to Cobain's apartment, where Hanna marked up a wall with the sentence "Kurt smells like Teen Spirit." Cobain took it as a compliment, thinking it was Hanna's interesting way of saying he still had the rebellious edge of an angry kid.

But Hanna was actually putting some arch humor to use – "Teen Spirit" was actually the rather insipid, niche-marketed brand name of an underarm deodorant for young women put out by the Mennen company. It wasn't until after Cobain had written, recorded, and released the song that he realized a trendy anti-perspirant had provided the title for his tune.

Musically, the song also had a specific moment of conception:

"We'd been practicing [with Grohl] for about three months," Cobain told David Fricke of *Rolling Stone*

smells like teen spirit

magazine in a January 1994 interview.

"We were waiting to sign to DGC, and Dave and I were living in Olympia and Krist was living in Tacoma. We were driving up to Tacoma every night for practice, trying to write songs. I was trying to write the ultimate pop song. I was basically trying to rip off the Pixies. I have to admit it. When I heard the Pixies for the first time, I connected with that band so heavily I should have been in that band – or at least in a Pixies cover band. We used their sense of dynamics, being soft and quiet and then loud and hard.

" 'Teen Spirit' was such a clichéd riff. It was so close to a Boston riff or 'Louie Louie'. When I came up with the guitar part, Krist looked at me and said, 'That is so ridiculous.' I made the band play it for an hour and a half."

The proximity of the chord changes in 'Teen Spirit' to those of the 1976 Boston hit 'More Than A Feeling' was remarked on frequently when the song was released. But, as would be the case again and again, knowing where Cobain might have borrowed from didn't diminish the inspired power of the track. Also much remarked upon was the perceived incoherence of the lyrics. The song was generally heard as an ironic rallying cry for thoroughly disaffected youth – an interpretation encouraged by the nightmarish high school pep rally depicted in the song's video. But even fans immediately grabbed by the song had trouble figuring out what exactly was being said.

Again, while Cobain's lyrics were terrifically evocative, they didn't necessarily stand up to a deep reading. But 'Teen Spirit' does seem to work as a glum study of what it feels like to be a reluctant part of an ugly group. The high-spirited energy of the music plays against the dementedly downcast words, beginning with Cobain's encouragement for some would-be revellers to "Load up on guns." The chorus seems to list what it takes to make for a spirited teen encounter: mulattos, albinos, a mosquito and Cobain's libido.

One of the lines that did clearly stand out, "Here we are now, entertain us," had a history as a Cobain entrance line. "That came from something I used to say every time I used to walk into a party to break the ice," Cobain told Fricke. "A lot of times when you're standing around with people in a room, it's really boring and uncomfortable. So it was, 'Well, here we are, entertain us. You invited us here.'"

Life gradually imitated art in a painful way for Cobain. As Nirvana became more and more popular and more fans began to embrace the cynical 'Teen Spirit' with energetically earnest teen spirit of their own, the song became more of a burden for him.

At some of Nirvana's final concerts, the band would pointedly leave the big hit that the screaming teens were clamoring for off their set list.

Despite the fan's appeals, 'Teen Spirit' was often omitted from the band's final shows.

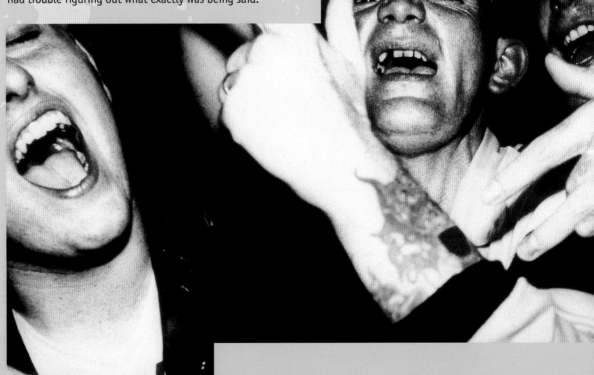

"Three fine youngsters from Seattle" – the video for 'In Bloom' saw the band poking fun at their sullen image.

in bloom

In one of three *Nevermind* songs to feature guns prominently in the lyrics, Cobain painted a thumbnail sketch of a character whose life consists of bad parenting and blissfully stupid rock n' roll escapism. Drawing on visions of some of the rock-loving, perpetually-stoned losers he'd grown up around in Aberdeen, Cobain describes a guy who's a bit past his "teen spirit" prime – he's now got some kids that he's hoping to "sell for food," which is no cause for heartache because, as he tells his companion, "we can have some more."

The character lives for the moments when he's swept away by a "pretty song" to which he'll sing-along. Maybe he'll even get happy enough to fire off his guns. The happiness isn't too deep though – the guy has no conception of what he's singing along to, and no self-awareness. In biblical syntax, he knows not what it means.

At the time Cobain wrote 'In Bloom', the kind of dumb rock fans he had in mind were still a bit of an oddity at Nirvana shows. But from the start he and the band had sometimes been approached by "rocker dudes" who liked Nirvana's loud catchy stuff without knowing, or caring, at all about what the music was trying to get at on any level other than one of rockin' out. But the song proved to be troublingly prophetic – by the time Nirvana was at the top of the charts, millions of people were coming to Nirvana shows to sing along while knowing not what it meant. The beauty of 'In Bloom' was that while it was a sly and satisfying condemnation of this kind of fandom, it was also an exciting enough rock tune to

engender mass sing-alongs. It managed to satisfy egghead ironists and blithe moshers with the same chorus.

The gun imagery from 'In Bloom' and other *Nevermind* songs was no great stretch of imagination for Cobain, who had grown up surrounded by gun owners in Aberdeen. In fact, Cobain wasn't aware he had used guns so prominently until he started to be questioned about it by interviewers after the release of *Nevermind*. Guns had in fact already played a tragic part in the Cobain family history. One of Kurt's great-uncles had died after shooting himself in the stomach in 1979, and another family member had killed himself in a similar fashion five years later.

In the studio, 'In Bloom' gave Dave Grohl a chance to shine apart from his thunderous drum work – he sang the achingly high harmonies that power the choruses.

The song took on a life apart from *Nevermind* when the band, with director Kevin Kerslake, came up with a particularly inspired video concept to accompany the track. Parodying early rock-on-TV programs such as *Hullabaloo*, the band performed with awkwardly slicked-back hair and matching suits, achieving a properly-dated, grainy look by being filmed through old-fashioned Kinescopes. Cobain enjoyed the humorous irony of having the band introduced in the video by a preening host (Doug Llewellyn of TV's *The People's Court*) who describes them as, "nice, decent, clean-cut young men."

The video shoot also had an effect on Nirvana fashion – Cobain liked the thick horn-rim glasses he wore while shooting the video so much that he kept them on for several months afterward.

come as you are

after the amazing mix of sharp guitar/drums onslaught and pure pop rush of 'Teen Spirit' and 'In Bloom', *Nevermind* abruptly shifted gears to the chilly feel and seemingly sub-aquatic guitar parts of 'Come As You Are'. The relaxed, almost graceful vibe of the music perfectly matches what was a unique and radical departure in the message of Cobain's lyrics. Instead of giving voice to outrage, indignation, disgust or self-loathing, the singer had decided to write a song of acceptance and invitation.

Cobain was acutely aware of social dynamics wherein a group sustains itself by making those outside the group objects of scorn and ridicule – he'd grown up feeling he was one of those excluded, ridiculed, misfit kids. But he felt that somewhere out there – in a better place where people listened to better records – there was a group he could fit into. He hoped he'd found that

group when he made his way into the punk rock world, but as Nirvana became a thriving entity on the Seattle scene, Cobain came to see that even "cool" scenes could be as vindictive and exclusive as the bunches of Aberdeen toughs who simply beat up weaker kids. He first railed against this kind of in-crowd small-mindedness on *Bleach*'s 'School'.

As he wrote for *Nevermind*, it occurred to Cobain that he was now in enough of a position of power, of "coolness," to be the one welcoming others into his own group. So, 'Come As You Are' sings out as an open, somewhat melancholy invitation to misfits everywhere. He also makes a point of assuring those he's addressing that he shouldn't be seen as a threat – in this song, he doesn't "have a gun." The song also made passing reference to the substance that had given the first album its title, when invitees are asked to come regardless of being covered in mud or "soaked in bleach."

This was one of several songs that had not been written when Vig met the band to record the Smart Studios demos. The first time the producer heard it

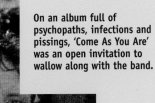

On an album full of psychopaths, infections and pissings, 'Come As You Are' was an open invitation to wallow along with the band.

was shortly before the *Nevermind* sessions began – it had been recorded crudely by the band on a boombox.

The video for 'Come As You Are' is notable in that it played on *Nevermind*'s central visual image – the submerged infant from the album's cover. The song also brought the band another round of legal hassles (following those surrounding the use of the name Nirvana). The band Killing Joke sued Nirvana, claiming that the central riff from 'Come As You Are' copied the central riff from their song 'Eighties'. Unlike the suits involving the band's name, this one didn't cost them much – Killing Joke lost the case.

breed

hurtling forward like an out-of-control big rig, 'Breed' gives *Nevermind* its finest moments of sheer, hair-tossing, riff-metal pleasure. The lyrics find Cobain growling about apathy, alienation, and lust gone flaccid, but the song had its genesis in a prescription drug. It was originally titled 'Imodium', and was written during Nirvana's first

European tour when they traveled in very close quarters with Sub Pop labelmates, TAD.

As they were getting their young label off the ground, co-owners Poneman and Pavitt of Sub Pop were wise to a truism of promotion – certain types of English and American bands always did better in their home countries after they had appeared in the press across the Atlantic. American acts, from Jimi Hendrix to the Ramones, had only been able to work up a major buzz at home after they'd performed across the sea, and the same had held for acts such as Britain's Police. Knowing that some rave reviews in the British press would give the Seattle scene a major jump start in the American press, Sub Pop invited some British journalists, including Everett True of *Melody Maker*, to check out the budding Northwest scene in 1989. The strategy paid off – the desired reviews appeared in the UK, and suddenly Kurt Cobain and a few other Seattlites were figures of international punk renown.

The British attention made the booking of a European tour logical, and, in October 1989, Nirvana and TAD set about taking Europe by van. The bands were excited, but good times were occasionally dimmed by the lack of elbow room in that van. Considering that Nirvana's bassist was the 6'7" Novoselic, and that Tad was fronted by the three hundred pound-plus TAD Doyle – it's not surprising that space in a modest Fiat van was at a premium. To complicate matters further, the hefty Doyle began suffering from terrible gastrointestinal problems, unable to get through a day without bouts of vomiting and/or diarrhea. The medicine he took to try to calm his perturbed guts was Imodium, which Cobain soon appropriated as a song title to go with a particularly powerful riff he'd come up with.

'Imodium' was one of the seven songs recorded by Butch Vig at the Smart Studios demo sessions in April 1990. Musically, it was already very close to the form it would take on *Nevermind*, but by the time the band got into its Sound City sessions a year later the anti-diarrhea agent had given way to 'Breed', and the lyrics had tightened into the song's minimal statements of boredom and dismay.

Cobain saw not sustenance but
swindle in organized religion.
A brief stay in a born-again
Christian household led to 'Breed'.

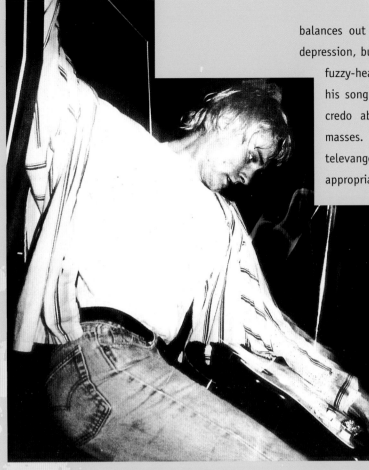

balances out the tremendous mood swings of manic depression, but can also reduce a patient to a state of fuzzy-headed neutrality. Cobain used the drug in his song title as a substitute for Karl Marx's old credo about religion being the opiate of the masses. In the era of cartoonishly soothing televangelists, Cobain felt that religion had more appropriately become the lithium of the masses.

There is at least a scrap or two of autobiography behind the writing of 'Lithium'. Cobain's parents, Don and Wendy, divorced in 1976 when Kurt was nine years old, and from that time on he never had a very stable home life. Though his mother received legal custody of Kurt, for the next several years he was shuttled back and forth between his parents. As the respective relationships between mother and son and father and son grew frayed

lithium

'Lithium' is Cobain's examination of the effects of organized religion on an unstable mind. There's nothing novel in the idea of a rock band taking on religion in a song – witness the Damned's 'Anti-Pope' – in fact, the punk screed against religious hypocrisy has become almost a cliché. What makes 'Lithium' so potent is Cobain's decision to work from inside – to sing as the person who's turning to God in order to help save a messed-up life and soothe a messed-up head. The first-person lyrics introduce us to a character who is troubled, very nearly insane and sustained only by a faith in God, but Cobain's lyrics – far from being a scathing indictment – are vaguely sympathetic. The fact that a song about God and madness is built on one of the sweetest melodies of the whole album makes it doubly effective.

As for the title, the substance lithium is a naturally occurring element, which turns up in combination with other substances to form a simple salt. Synthetic lithium has been widely prescribed as a treatment for manic-depressive disorders, though its precise action on the brain is still not understood. It effectively

and difficult, young Cobain looked for other homes to take refuge in. At the beginning of 1985, Kurt was on particularly bad terms with his mother – who was remarried and pregnant – and his father, who was bitterly disappointed that Kurt had not only failed in high school, but had also shown no interest in a career in the U.S. Navy.

Cobain moved in briefly with the family of a friend called Jesse Reed. The Reeds, though not especially delighted with their son's choice of companion, provided Kurt with food and shelter for a month, requesting only that their house-guest respect their religious beliefs – they were both born-again Christians. From those few weeks of having an inside look at a working-class, fundamentalist Christian household, Cobain drew inspiration for the odd character who sings 'Lithium'.

Fighting off the horror: 'Polly' was often Cobain's single moment of terrifying calm in otherwise explosive Nirvana shows.

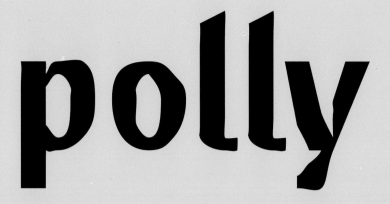

polly

obain didn't often pluck song ideas wholesale from the newspapers he read, but occasionally a story moved him enough that he answered it with a song. Such was the case with the true-life child abuse scenario he had transformed into the troubling 'Paper Cuts', and it was also the case with 'Polly'. In 1987, Seattle papers followed the awful story of a local crime: a young girl had been abducted at gunpoint by a man named Gerald Friend after she attended a punk-rock show at the Community World Theater in Tacoma. She was taken to the trailer Friend lived in, where he bound her up, raped her repeatedly and tortured her with whips, razors and a blowtorch.

She was finally able to escape when he took her out in his car to run some errands. Friend was subsequently arrested and convicted, and remains in prison.

Cobain wanted to capture the horror of this incident in a song, but the very real horror behind the story made it difficult for him to feel completely comfortable with it. 'Polly' was first developed along with *Bleach*-era material, and the song went through several transformations, sometimes sung starkly as a mostly acoustic song, sometimes bashed out in electric form. Cobain winnowed down his lyrical ideas until he finally captured the impressionistic, but nonetheless harrowing, confessional from the rapist's point of view, which is what makes 'Polly' such a stand out song. It was recorded during sessions for the 'Blew' EP, and at the Smart Studios demo sessions. It was the Smart version, gently strummed on a beaten up acoustic guitar, that the band, and producer Vig, felt fully captured the horror of the crime in a frightening and movingly understated fashion. That demo track was simply re-mixed for *Nevermind* to retain its stark power, in contrast to the pop luster of the rest of the album.

In the mad tumble of Nirvana concerts, 'Polly' was frequently a show-stopping moment of chilling quiet. The song's subdued intensity was such that when no less a song writer than Bob Dylan had the opportunity to see the band perform in New York, it was 'Polly' that led him to describe Nirvana as a band with "guts" and to say of Cobain, "the kid has heart."

The song came hideously full circle when, in 1991, a pair of thugs raped a young girl while singing 'Polly'. Cobain addressed that incident in the liner notes to *Incesticide*, in which he referred to the two rapists as, "two wastes of sperm and eggs." He went on to say;

"I have a hard time carrying on knowing there are plankton like that in our audience. Sorry to be so anally P.C., but that's the way I feel."

Interestingly enough the band did not look upon this brutal incident as a reason to jettison 'Polly' from performances. Instead, Cobain reclaimed the tune, and continued to include it in concerts – its doubled real-life inspirations making it an even more starkly affecting work.

t he most straightforwardly "punk" track on *Nevermind*, 'Territorial Pissings' takes a swipe, with its title, at scenester cliquishness and displays of rock n' roll machismo. Lyrically, the three-chord thrasher charges into slightly different territory, offering up some of Cobain's fortune cookie-sized takes on life in general. The song offers some truisms on paranoia and feminine wisdom along with screams begging for an escape into a better future.

One bit of lyric that had some personal resonance for Cobain was the opening line, in which he thought back to when he was an "alien." In Michael Azerrad's *Come As You Are*, Cobain explained to the writer where the extraterrestrial image came from – Cobain constantly fantasized as a child that he was a creature from another planet. "I wanted to be from another planet really bad," he explained. "Every night I used to talk to my real parents and my real family in the skies. I knew that there were thousands of other alien babies dropped off and they were all over and I'd met quite a few of them." Several psychological texts refer to this fantasy as a very common one among sensitive or highly intelligent children who find themselves in adverse, non-supportive circumstances.

The lyrics of 'Territorial Pissings' didn't need to cohere much – what moves the song forward is its implosive energy. Part of the vibe of the finished track came from a recording technique that Cobain had used back on the Fecal Matter cassette he recorded at his aunt's house in Aberdeen. Instead of plugging his guitar into an amp and miking that to record his part, he plugged the guitar – against the wishes of Butch Vig – directly into the recording console. The song was

recorded in one hyper-kinetic, over-the-top take. Actually, a "take two" would have been impossible – as one can hear on *Nevermind*, Cobain's voice gives out before the track is over.

The song also gave Novoselic his only showcase as a Nirvana vocalist. As the tape was rolling, he was asked to sing something to introduce the track. He tore into a hearty, off-key chorus from the Youngbloods' 1967 single 'Get Together'. The song, written by Dino Valente of Quicksilver Messenger Service, had been a pop hit when it was re-released by the Youngbloods on the heels of their *Elephant Mountain* album. It was also familiar to children of the 1970s, when it was appropriated for use in public service television spots promoting goodwill and neighborliness. Novoselic's heightened delivery of the song's peace-and-love sentiments is clearly meant to be a comic aside, but he later admitted he meant the 1960s band no ill will.

"It just kind of happened. I wanted to put some kind of corny hippie idealism in ['Territorial Pissings']. But it really wasn't that thought into. I like that Youngbloods song."

'Territorial Pissings' came to serve an important role in Nirvana concerts. The band had long enjoyed the pleasure of smashing the hell out of their instruments during shows. Here was the perfect, snarling tune to facilitate the demolition of guitars and drums at the end of a set. The song was also pulled out on occasion as a "screw you" to television producers and media types who the band didn't like. If the band felt cheated by a television program they'd agreed to appear on, they'd skip whatever "hit" they'd been asked to play and serve up a thoroughly contemptuous 'Territorial Pissings'.

territorial pissings

When I was an alien: a longstanding
Cobain fantasy of extraterrestrial
heritage was part of the inspiration
for 'Territorial Pissings'.

drain you

From a very early age, Kurt was fascinated by the images of childhood, especially babies, in artwork. Many of the paintings and drawings he did as a kid depicted babies or baby-like aliens in various oddly juxtaposed surroundings. By the time he'd

Two babies: drawn together during the recording of *Nevermind*, Kurt Cobain and Courtney Love were married shortly after the album went to number one.

left high school and moved into his first apartment in Aberdeen, his fascination had grown strong enough, and macabre enough, that he decorated the place with bloodied, plastic baby dolls in tiny nooses. He eventually took to buying modeling clay, sculpting his own baby figures and baking the forms in his oven. Later he became even more fascinated with the anatomically accurate models of babies, fetuses and body parts that could be bought from medical catalogs and surgical supply shops.

This obsession with the birth process and the bodily fluids remained with Cobain – the apartments and homes he shared with Courtney Love were full of the baby dolls and medical models that Cobain had continued to acquire. He ended up, after all, titling an album *In Utero*, wherein a listener couldn't travel far at all before skidding through a pool of one bodily fluid or another. But it was on *Nevermind* that he first incorporated his infatuation with babies and body function into a song and, surprisingly, ended up with a song that was one of his most tender and oddly romantic.

Cobain had been through a few serious romances by the time he was writing for *Nevermind*, and in 'Drain You' he tried to capture the heady, two-bodies-becoming-one buzz that exists at the start of any passionate love affair. This was done by describing a pair of babies who are lying next to each other and becoming intimately acquainted with each other – they pass food back and forth between their mouths in a delicious – and nutritious – kiss, and generously "drain" each other of infection. While most of Cobain's songs were made up of abstract phrases brought together by the power of the singer's mood and the band's music, here he expertly follows through with the conceit of the song. The strange babies perfectly illustrate the feelings of lovers who want to be so close that they are inside each other, and also the narcissistic feelings of love for oneself simply because one is in love.

"I think there are so many other songs that I've written that are as good, if not better, than 'Teen Spirit'," Cobain told *Rolling Stone* magazine in 1994. "Like 'Drain You'. That's definitely as good as 'Teen Spirit'. I love the lyrics, and I never get tired of playing it." He then added a final caveat: "Maybe if it was as big as 'Teen Spirit', I wouldn't like it as much."

Aside from being a lyrical stand-out on *Nevermind*, 'Drain You' also gave a taste of what the band could pull off as a trio of players – the song's pounding, crescendoing instrumental break is a musical highlight of the album. Cobain was unavoidably thrust into the spotlight as the "face" and "voice" of Nirvana, but 'Drain You' is one of those tracks that makes it clear just how powerful Nirvana was as a band.

'Drain You' meant as
much to Cobain as 'Teen
Spirit' did to his fans.

49

the loping bass line that Novoselic uses to kick off 'Lounge Act' doesn't sound like it's heralding a piece of cocktail jazz, but the band joked that the tune's bouncy feeling had the retro-cheese swing of some mediocre hotel-lounge covers band. So, what began as a lyricless jam was given a smirking title that stuck. But by the time Cobain had completed the lyrics to the tune, shortly before it was recorded at the Smart sessions, the words bore little relation to the title.

When Kurt left Aberdeen to move in with girlfriend Tracy Marander in Olympia, he was just beginning to come into his own as a writer, musician, and artist – just beginning to realize that some of the aspects of his personality that had made him a put-upon misfit up until then were actually his ticket to a better world. As he became increasingly ambitious toward his music, he was faced with a personal dilemma. While Marander was exceptionally supportive – personally and financially – of Cobain's artistic and musical efforts, his compulsion and dedication to those efforts made it difficult for him

Northwest in the early 1990s. Vail was also the drummer with the band Bikini Kill.

The energy and passion that Vail and other "Riot Grrls" brought to their music and beliefs was a key impetus in getting Cobain to take his own music seriously enough to make Nirvana a contender on the Seattle scene. Ironically, it was after Nirvana's breakthrough that the Seattle/Olympia scene became energized to the point that Bikini Kill itself, and other "Riot Grrl" bands, got their music out on their own records. (Bikini Kill's self-titled EP, released in 1992 by Olympia's Kill Rock Stars label, was one of the movement's most powerful missives.)

On *Nevermind*, 'Lounge Act' ends with a bit of studio playfulness. The band, unable to come up with an ending they were completely happy with, simply slowed down the tape machine to create a groaning de-crescendo.

lounge act

to be a "good boyfriend" by any conventional standards.

Without playing on specifics, Cobain looked back at the feeling of having loyalties split between love and art in 'Lounge Act'. Although the song is not without sympathy for the person the singer is addressing, it rails against the smothering security of a relationship that is closing off a couple from the world at large, which one half of that couple wishes to explore more fully. The song also makes oblique reference to those on the Olympia scene whom Cobain felt had inspired him and validated his work. The "friend who makes me feel," who shows up in the chorus, is probably Tobi Vail, a girlfriend of Cobain's who was a pivotal presence in the "Riot Grrl" movement that took hold in the

stay away

'**S**tay Away' was the *Nevermind* track with the longest history – its basic riff had been first used by Cobain when he recorded material for his Fecal Matter tape. Cobain hung on to the riff, and developed it into a full piece of guitar music that he liked, but he put the lyrics through some big changes before he felt he had the song he was after.

The misfit was now a superstar. The music was still righteous, but post-*Nevermind* fame was a heavy burden on Cobain.

Though Cobain frequently downplayed the importance of his lyrics, he was, in fact, a lover of the written word who at times worked very hard on his own creations. Wherever he slept, there were sure to be a few spiral notebooks nearby. (It was Cobain's habit to fill pages with lyrics, poems and random thoughts before he went to sleep.) Once he'd found a basic idea, a simple rhyme or even just a title that he felt worthy of pursuing, lyrics would often go through change after change. Many of the songs on *Nevermind* had at one point contained several different potential verses and/or choruses, and would only take final shape when recording deadlines forced Cobain to become a serious editor of his own work.

'Stay Away' was originally titled 'Pay to Play'. That title made reference to an ugly custom that had begun in the mid-1980s among rock clubs, when glam-metal bands were the rage. Rather than booking a band and paying them a flat fee or a percentage of the door, club owners began charging bands for time on stage. Usually the system worked by forcing bands to buy a large block of tickets to their own show at a set price. It was then the band's responsibility to sell the tickets – with the understanding that they needed to mark up the price if they wished to make a profit. While the world of club-level economics had never been without injustices, the pay-to-play system was particularly heinous in that it valued marketing and name recognition over any musical value.

As the song's lyrics were transformed, they moved away from a direct confrontation of the pay-to-play issue, but remained a strong condemnation of a misguided rock n' roll scene. At a time when Guns n' Roses and Mötley Crüe were ostensibly setting the standards for what rock music should be, Cobain screamed that he'd rather be "dead than cool." His ragged-voiced "stay away"s are commands to the scene he wants no part of, advice to the unsuspecting listener and vows of personal resolve. It's also quite possible that his reference to "poison skin" is a dig at what he saw as one of the most grotesque rock n' roll success stories of the day – that of LA's Poison.

The song, in its original 'Pay to Play' form, appeared on a DGC Rarities album that was released in 1994.

on a plain

'**O**n a Plain' blasts out of *Nevermind* as one of Nirvana's finest high-energy blends of rock power and sing-along pop-craft, and contains one of the finest slogans a narcissist could hope for – I love myself better than you. But for all the evident craft and the several standout turns of phrase in the song, it's not a song with very much on its mind. In fact, it's a kind of meta-pop tune – a song about trying to write a song. Cobain begins the song by telling the listener he'll start off without any words – and he was speaking the plain truth.

Often, when the reality of committing *Nevermind*'s lyrics to record kicked in, Cobain would take the time to write and re-write in the studio, usually bringing all other production work to a complete halt. Unhappy with the notes he'd accumulated for 'On a Plain', Cobain sat down minutes before singing the song and furiously scribbled out the lyrics that ended up on the album. He was able to get the song done quickly by turning writers block into some winning couplets. He sings that it's time to be unclear, and that he needs to write lines that don't make sense. In the bridge section, Cobain was aware of having patterned the music after something that he vaguely recalled having heard before, so the appropriate lyric was "Somewhere I have heard this before." Use of the line "Don't quote me on that" stemmed from a running studio joke in which that line had come to be used as an all purpose addenda when answering any mundane question.

A few nuggets of autobiography turn up as Cobain sings of his mother and "black sheep" but, as he makes clear in the final verse, he is discouraging deep analysis – he simply wants to get the song sung so "I can go home."

What the hell am I trying to say? The feelings Cobain was trying to get across were absolutely clear, even if his words weren't.

nevermind

Hard comforts – the chilly dreamscape of 'Something In the Way' was based on Cobain's period of homelessness.

something in the way

nevermind's most evocative track grew from, and furthered, a key piece of Cobain legend. At the end of 1985, with no job prospects in sight and with several month's rent owed on an apartment he'd been sharing with his friend, Jesse Reed, Cobain became homeless. With some bare level of subsistence afforded by food stamps, Cobain took whatever shelter he could find. Sometimes that meant spending entire days in the Aberdeen library. At night, he might crash at Dale Crover's house – sleeping on the porch if he didn't wish to disturb the occupants. Or he might get a few hours sleep in Chris Novoselic's van. When he did not want to rely on the generosity of his friends, he set up a small encampment beneath the North Aberdeen

endless, nameless

Listeners who went about their business after hearing the twelve listed tracks of *Nevermind* without turning off the CD player received a noisy jolt a little over nine minutes after the end of 'Something in the Way'. The band included a bonus, untitled thirteenth track on the album. This track eventually came to be known as 'Endless, Nameless' and served as a generic name for the monumental pastiches of sonic decay that would close many Nirvana concerts.

Bridge, over the Wishkah river, and lived a tramp's life there.

Cobain may have lived that life for only a few weeks at most, but the notion that he had been a homeless drifter before finding sanctuary in the punk-rock world became a part of the Nirvana story as the band got popular in the area. In 'Something In the Way', written shortly before the *Nevermind* sessions, Cobain paints a moving, though self-admittedly exaggerated view of his life under that bridge. The "something" of the title is never made explicit – it might be a way of describing personal weaknesses not fully understood, though it also may well be Aberdeen and the no-future existences he saw rooted all around him.

The song's delicate mood made it the most difficult one to capture in the studio. Pumped-up band versions were not capturing the spirit Cobain was after, so producer Vig asked him to demonstrate on an acoustic guitar how he thought the song should be played. Cobain came into the producer's control room and began to strum and sing. Vig realized that this was the take that should be recorded and so he quickly set up microphones, shut down the rest of the studio and recorded Cobain's parts while the singer played on the control-room couch. The rest of the band took their cue from Cobain's subdued guitar and added their parts later. The cello work of Kirk Canning added some final, properly somber, tones to the arrangement.

Things were not going well during the recording of the delicately crafted 'Lithium' at one session, and Cobain decided to loosen up the proceedings by taking a break from his song and cranking up instead with some thoroughly senseless guitar noise. Novoselic and Grohl dived into the noise-jam with relish and, as the band indulged in some cathartic improvisation, Vig got it all on tape. The sounds were, in fact, so cathartic that Cobain was moved to smash his guitar up in the studio. This can be heard at the end of the track as a series of bangs that end with some high-pitched feedback.

The band decided to mix the song down and find a place for it on *Nevermind*. The decision to hide it was Cobain's. As a young Beatles fan, he'd loved the musical mystery that the band created through false starts, trick endings and acts of manipulating the very media they were working in – such as the way 'Her Majesty' was suddenly cut off at the end of *Abbey Road*. CDs had been around for a while, but were just then starting to be derided as an artistically and aesthetically unsatisfying format. Cobain decided to bring a little vinyl-era playfulness into the digital age with 'Endless, Nameless', and it wasn't long before every self-respecting "alternative" band was hiding a bonus track somewhere at the end of their CDs.

When *Nevermind* was first released, 'Endless, Nameless' turned out to be a little too well hidden. A technical miscommunication resulted in it being left off the first pressing of the album.

incesticide

The oddities, rarities and cover tunes of Incesticide charted the metamorphosis of Nirvana's sound from brain-chop punk to bona fide grunge and angst-pop.

irvana's second release on the DGC label played out as a scruffy, home-grown flipside to *Nevermind*. While that breakthrough album presented the band's talents in a work that was strikingly polished – some naysayers said overly manicured – the bunch of demos, singles and odds and sods that made up *Incesticide* presented the group without sweetening. While, for many fans, *Nevermind* was a compelling, chart-scaling juggernaut that seemed to have steamed in from nowhere, *Incesticide* offered the chance for those fans to study up on what path these Nirvana fellows had taken on their way to world domination. Here it was possible to hear Cobain and the band's growth pre-'Teen Spirit', – from Gang of Four and Scratch Acid-echoing art-punk constructions to proto-grunge Sub Pop metalisms and on toward what *Nevermind* had revealed – music almost revolutionary in its mix of rock muscle and pop smarts led by the voice of a uniquely talented song writer.

While perhaps *Incesticide* did not offer up the hour's worth of sheer, exhilarating listening pleasure that *Nevermind* did, and didn't hit with the darkly unified force of *Bleach*, its highlights – 'Sliver', 'Been A Son', 'Aneurysm' – were remarkable, and its curios – Devo covers, early demos – were insightful enough to remain engaging through repeat listens. The record also gave fans a chance to rate the work of the four different

drummers who recorded with Nirvana. (Dave Grohl wins fairly easily here – the exponential leap in the band's power once he took to the drum throne is astonishing.)

Incesticide was released in December 1992, and much had happened in the twelve months since *Nevermind* had flown to the top of the pop charts. After something of a whirlwind romance – a romance in which every gesture of mutual affection had been excitedly dissected by the press – Kurt and Courtney Love had decided to get married. The ceremony took place on February 24, 1992, on a cliff overlooking Waikiki beach. The service was performed by a female non-denominational minister and was attended by Dave Grohl and a few Nirvana employees.

August of that year brought the best and worst of news to Mr. and Mrs. Cobain. On August 18, the couple had a daughter – Frances Bean Cobain, named after actress Frances Farmer and the child's legume-like appearance in an early sonogram. But, just prior to Frances's birth, an article by journalist Lynn Hirschberg had appeared in *Vanity Fair* magazine in which Courtney Love seemed to indicate that she and Kurt had been using heroin while she was pregnant. The ensuing storm of negative press and public ill will that the couple encountered was not only unpleasant, but punishing – the baby was briefly taken away from them by Los Angeles County child welfare authorities until the couple proved that they could act as responsible parents. It turned out that Love had stopped using heroin very early on in the pregnancy, and the drugs had seemingly had no affect on Frances, who was healthy and normal. The baby's father, however, was far from healthy and his continuing drug use and suicidal tendencies were beginning to wreak serious havoc on his body, his family, his band, his friendships and his music.

By the end of the month, Nirvana – with a freshly detoxed Cobain – was on tour again and the group headlined that summer's Reading Festival. One year before the band had, for all intents and purposes, announced itself as a force to be reckoned with. At the 1991 Reading Festival, Nirvana had stormed the stage and delivered a blistering, fiercely triumphant set. At the 1992 Festival, the mood was, at first, decidedly less upbeat. Playing off the continuing rumors and hypotheses about the state of his health, Cobain made his entrance at Reading in a hospital smock and a wheelchair. Once out of his chair on the festival stage, and with the band fired up, Cobain demonstrated what would be the central tenet of his existence – despite the drugs, the self-loathing, the insecurities and whatever other negatives Cobain's small frame was said to

contain, the music remained magnificent.

By the time of *Incesticide*'s release in December, the band had become a couple of things that it had never even considered back when they were playing shows for eight people at the Central Tavern in Seattle.

Firstly, they were tabloid fodder. With the Reagan-era's dunder-headed "Just Say No" anti-drug campaigns still echoing in America, Kurt and Courtney became the country's favorite hatable, drug-abusing rock n' roll couple. The couple's spats with Axl Rose backstage at September's MTV Video Music Awards didn't do much to shore up their "alternative" credibility. To many who had first rooted for Nirvana as a small-town band-done-good, they now seemed to be – at least Cobain seemed to be – a creature of rock n' roll excess, capable of as much ego-driven behavior as those rock stars the band had once professed to hate.

Secondly, the band had become associated with a moment of rock fashion that quickly ballooned from honest local custom to monstrous marketing movement – that is to say, they were seen as the harbingers of "Grunge." The word had been around for at least a decade – singer Mark Arm of Mudhoney had used it in

Where they came from: *Incesticide* documented the transformation from the grungesters of *Bleach* to the punk-poppers of *Nevermind*.

print in 1980 as a put-down of his own band at the time (Mr. Epp and the Calculations). The word had also been kicked around in Sub Pop press releases of the late 1980s, again as an almost ironically back-handed compliment. But, post-*Nevermind*, suddenly the word had a capital "G." The sound was laid claim to by every guitarist with a distortion unit and the look went from being one born of working-class necessity to one that was instantly purchasable at the mall. Copycat haircuts, clothing and recording contracts had come in the wake of Beatlemania, but that band had been slightly better equipped, or at least more willing, to work on two levels – giving itself up as happy product to screaming teenyboppers, while offering deeper satisfaction and craftier sounds to those who wished to hear them. While *Nevermind* was an ingenious sneak-attack on the

Cobain addressed Nirvana fans directly in the liner notes of *Incesticide*, settling some scores and making some harsh observations.

mainstream, Kurt Cobain's conflicted nature and ever-fragile sensibility meant that maintaining that attack at that level would be impossible. He would not happily or willingly be crowned King of Grunge.

In December 1992, just in time to remind listeners that Nirvana had been a band before it was a cultural phenomenon, *Incesticide* was released. Culled from demos, EPs, compilation tracks and BBC recordings, the record was a one-disc lesson in Nirvana history. But perhaps even more striking than the music on *Incesticide* were the liner notes that Cobain penned for the album. Taking it upon himself to do some score settling, he enumerated the rewards and burdens of being the main guy in the world's biggest band, and did so with alternating flashes of wry humor and unrestrained rage.

On the plus side, Cobain found reward in, among other things, tracking down the first Raincoats album, receiving artwork from Daniel Johnston, being asked to produce a Melvins record and touring with groups such as Sonic Youth, Shonen Knife, the Breeders, the Jesus Lizard and Hole. Cobain railed against those who had painted Courtney Love as some sort of "Dragon Lady" and those who had assumed he was dumb enough to be tricked into marriage. He asked Nirvana fans who were racist, homophobic or misogynist to simply stop being Nirvana fans – "Leave us the fuck alone! Don't come to our shows and don't buy our records." He also condemned the two rapists who had misappropriated his song 'Polly' while committing their crime.

The liner notes were a grand statement – a sort of textbook act of rock star-ism, but one couldn't accuse Cobain of using the notes to puff up the importance of Nirvana's music. At one point he stated, "I'll be the first to admit that we're the 90's version of Cheap Trick or the Knack but the last to admit that it hasn't been rewarding."

dive

Sound of the future: 'Dive' was the only Butch Vig-produced track on *Incesticide*.

'dive' was originally released in September 1990 as the B-side to Nirvana's final double-sided single for Sub Pop – their final Sub Pop release was a split single with the Fluid. In some ways – sonically at least – this song perfectly wraps up the band's relationship with its original label. Though just about everyone in Seattle would eventually come to hate the term "grunge," when it was first being bandied about it referred to the sound of tunes like 'Dive' – thick, dirty guitar, menacing bass, ham-handed drums and vocals of indeterminate agony. It was a sound that had been developed, for the most part, quite naturally by its earliest practitioners – the principle of grunge was more a result of less-than-dazzling instrumental prowess and cheap equipment than any self-conscious esthetic.

On the other hand, Pavitt and Poneman of Sub Pop didn't end up with a "Sub Pop sound" entirely by accident – they did push somewhat to bring out the grungier side of their acts in look, sound and press. Poneman's calmly resolute guidance had ensured that *Bleach* was truer to the Sub Pop spirit than it might have been if Nirvana had pursued its artier tendencies toward psycho-noise. So, post-*Bleach* and conscious that he was writing for a band recording for a label with a fairly specific sound, Cobain had come up with 'Dive'. The song represents nicely what was perhaps coolest about grunge at first – it was music delivered with punk intensity, but also unafraid to scream out its love and allegiance to classic, heavy metal rock n' roll. As Cobain explained to the *Chicago Tribune* in a 1991 article:

"Around 1985, '86, the hardcore scene seemed exhausted to us... It was boring, so we just started accepting the fact that we liked the music that we grew up on: Alice Cooper, the MC 5, Kiss. It was almost taboo to admit something like that in '85, but we grew our hair long

and said, 'Fuck what everybody else thinks, we're going to do what we want'... We're paying homage to all the bands we loved as kids, and we haven't denied the punk-rock energy that inspired us as teenagers."

The fat, mid-tempo beat and heavy rockin' guitar riff of 'Dive' illustrate exactly what Cobain was talking about. Thematically, the song also straddles classic rock and punk rock – it's a come-on sung by someone who wants to be left alone.

'Dive' was first recorded with Jason Everman as a part of the band, when Nirvana recorded a radio performance at Evergreen State College in Olympia. (This session yielded Everman's only recorded work with the band ever released – a cover of Kiss's 'Do You Love Me', which later appeared on a tribute album called *Hard to Believe*, released by C/Z, a Seattle indie label.) The version of 'Dive' that appears on *Incesticide* was recorded when the band – Kurt, Krist and Chad Channing – first worked with producer Butch Vig. They recorded a 10-song demo at his Smart Studios in Madison, Wisconsin, in April 1990. Much of what was recorded that day ('Breed', 'Lithium', 'Stay Away') would only spring fully to life when the band re-connected with Vig for the *Nevermind* sessions. But, owing Sub Pop some material, they picked off their "demo" version of 'Dive' for use as a single.

It's interesting, when listening to 'Dive', to keep in mind that it's the only Vig-produced track on *Incesticide*. The sound of the song points grungily backward to Sub Pop, but the production already hints at the sonic size the band would assume shortly on *Nevermind*.

sliver

mid-1990 was a curious time for Nirvana. They considered *Bleach* to be a personal – if not commercial – success, touring had given them a worldwide reputation as a band to watch and a music industry buzz was growing louder by the week. But when Kurt and Krist decided to let Chad Channing go, the old drummer problems resumed. Who would be that all-important drum-bashing third of the Nirvana triad? The answer, for one B-side and one tremendously pivotal Seattle show at the Motor Sports International venue, was Dan Peters, who had come from the temporarily defunct Mudhoney, and would go on to the Screaming Trees and back to Mudhoney after his few days with Nirvana.

Peters's brief stint happened to coincide with the band's need to record an A-side for its final Sub Pop single, but, while it's Peters's drumming that powers 'Sliver', it's Tad Doyle's drums that are being played. In July of 1990, Tad was working in the studio with Jack Endino. It was during these sessions that Cobain, with Endino's cooperation, decided to employ some guerrilla recording tactics. The plan was that when Tad took a dinner break, Nirvana would dash into the studio and use the downtime to bash out the fundamentals of their track on Tad's equipment. Doyle was not at all happy with the idea, but finally acquiesced when Endino assured him that he would allow none of Nirvana's customary instrument-bashing while they were in the studio. So, on July 11, 1990, while Tad supped, Nirvana bashed out most of 'Sliver' in a little over an hour.

The song seems a more delicate thing than its recording background might indicate, because the frightening child's-eye tale it relates is so resonant. Here, truly, was the first track in which Cobain demonstrated his full, astonishing talents as a song writer. In just a few words set against an exhilarating mix of grinding guitar and sunny, sing-along melody, Cobain captured – and made a listener re-experience – all the night-terrors of an unhappy childhood. With a simple pleading chorus ("Grandma take me home") sung in first a deadened, exhausted voice and then screamed, Cobain brought it all back – the feelings of being small, powerless and at the mercy of people who don't understand what you want. Even those with the happiest of childhoods might remember times when the world, and the people around them, seemed all wrong.

Unfortunately for Cobain, this song – though not autobiographical – required little imagination. His parents' divorce and the shuttling between relatives he had endured as a result were the key

events that turned his relatively happy early childhood into one of insecurity and despondency.

"Up until I was nine I felt I could become a rock star or astronaut or the president," Cobain told Robert Hilburn of the *Los Angeles Times* in a 1993 interview. "I had total freedom and a lot of love and support from my family – at least on my Mom's side. [After the divorce] I was embarrassed and became really detached and quiet.

My mom would take me to school and I wouldn't even look kids in the eye. I knew everyone knew that I only had one parent. That isn't probably a big deal in a big town, but it is in a small town... I was a seriously depressed kid. Every night at one point I'd go to bed bawling my head off. I used to try to make my head explode by holding my breath, thinking if I blew up my head, they'd be sorry."

Not a happy family: Cobain set some panicky childhood feelings to a brilliant pop tune with 'Sliver'.

A triumph of low self-
esteem: Cobain's lyrics,
like those in 'Stain',
often came from the
veiwpoint of a defeated,
unhinged soul.

stain

early on as a song writer, Cobain was playing with opposites – jumps between loud and soft, harmony and dissonance, pop feel and punk feel were all put to effective use in Nirvana's music. Lyrically, his songs also usually played with one of two points of view – either he was gazing at something with a contemptuous eye, or gazing at himself with a contemptuous eye. 'Stain' falls quite solidly into the latter category. It's almost a throwaway tune for the band – just a squarely rocking riff, a thrice repeated verse about how horrible the singer is and an oddly gentle chorus in which said singer claims to be the titular blotch. Basically, 'Stain' rips along as a minor addenda to *Bleach*'s 'Negative Creep'.

When Cobain had his own apartment, first in Aberdeen and then in Olympia, his housekeeping and hygiene were legendarily lax. The living spaces became sprawling monuments of filth, random personal effects and Cobain's favored oven-baked clay-covered baby dolls. In Olympia, as he and the band began to develop a reputation in the music scene, Cobain was seen as something of a comical "monk" figure – a man without customary guy-in-a-band desires, who was content to sit at home in the mess of his own making when not out pursuing band business. 'Stain' was written as a response to those Olympians who, in mainly friendly fashion, poked fun at Cobain's manner of living. In the song, he cops the plea to being one who doesn't fuck, read, sleep or leave the house, because he is saddled with "bad luck."

'Stain' was recorded in the summer of 1989 as part of the band's 'Blew' EP and released on Tupelo records. Sub Pop was most adept at putting out singles and EPs – the band had had to push a bit to get Bruce Pavitt and Jonathan Poneman to agree to *Bleach* being a full album – so it was quite natural for the band to follow up its full-length release with something shorter on the Sub Pop-related Tupelo imprint. There was no bad blood with Jack Endino, but the band decided to try a new room and a new personality and so recorded the EP at Seattle's Music Source studios with producer Steve Fisk. Music Source was a bit of a step up for Nirvana – a clean, 24-track studio – and Fisk was recognized as an important figure in the Olympia and eastern Washington music scenes. He had spent several years working at Velvetone studio in Ellensburg, WA, where he had recorded or worked with Beat Happening, Girl Trouble, Screaming Trees, Soundgarden and several hardcore bands, as well as putting together his own sonic collage albums of electronic weirdness tossed together with bits of television shows and movie dialogue.

Fisk had initially been unimpressed with an early Nirvana club performance he witnessed – he was particularly bothered by Jason Everman's hair-tossing, macho-metal mannerisms. But after Bruce Pavitt made a point of sending a copy of *Bleach* Fisk's way, the producer realized there was solid talent to work with in the group and gladly took on the project. In addition to 'Stain', Fisk recorded 'Even In His Youth', an electric version of 'Polly' and 'Been A Son'. When the 'Blew' EP was released, it paired 'Blew' and 'Love Buzz' from *Bleach* with the Fisk recordings of 'Stain' and 'Been a Son'.

been a son

A long with 'Sliver', 'Been A Son' stands as one of the earliest indications that Cobain was someone capable of deeply affecting song writing and masterly popcraft. While Cobain had kept some of his poppier influences to himself in Nirvana's earliest days, once *Bleach* was done and the band began to be asked about favorite records in interviews, Cobain made no secret of his love of the Beatles and John Lennon's songs in particular – though it has been suggested by some that musically, Cobain's sense of composition was a lot closer to Paul McCartney's. In 'Been a Son', one is basically hearing those childhood Beatles records blooming into something new through Cobain – the song seems to have sprung from some indeterminate spot between *Rubber Soul* and *Revolver*.

The song also represents one of the earliest and most concise statements from Cobain on the issues of sex and gender – issues that he would continue to speak out on. The burly, mill-town machismo of Aberdeen had worked as a kind of vaccine on Cobain – throughout his career he would be sickened by displays of high-testosterone masculinity (vicious moshing, for example) and always seemed to take enjoyment from shocking interviewers, acquaintances and the world at large with displays of cross-gender dressing and behavior. Here was a male rock star who could be seen in lingerie and nighties, who frequently wore dresses to interviews not for glam value, camp value or comic value, but because he said simply that they were comfortable garments and he had a right to wear them. His anti-macho philosophy

was given a reverse-angle view in 'Been A Son', in which a put-upon daughter's worth goes so unnoticed that she might as well have died at birth if she wasn't going to be born with a penis.

The song evokes situations such as those in China, where female fetuses are routinely aborted because daughters are thought to be of no value. As he came of age, Cobain became aware of the less murderous but no less devastating attitudes toward womanhood and femininity that existed all around him in Aberdeen. In a 1992 *Option* magazine interview with Gina Arnold, he spoke of his earliest feelings of crossing gender lines in his hometown.

"I was a life-guard, and I taught pre-school kids how to swim, and I worked at the YMCA and did day care, and I babysat during my teenage years. Which was all kind of a strange thing in Aberdeen, because mostly males don't babysit that much, and sometimes when I was sitting and the lady's date would come over, he'd have this weird reaction when he saw me – like it wasn't right or something."

The song was originally recorded for, and released on, the 'Blew' EP, but the version that appears on *Incesticide* comes from a radio session that the band – with Dave Grohl having replaced Chad Channing – taped for British disc-jockey Mark Goodier while they were in London during a European tour at the end of 1991.

Cobain paid tribute to the brainy proponents of de-evolution on *Incesticide*.

turnaround

In October 1990, Nirvana, with spanking-new drummer Dave Grohl, made a second trip to Britain for a series of shows. They also arranged for a second recording session with legendary radio figure John Peel – they'd recorded for him during their first European tour, which had featured Chad Channing on drums. The tour was in support of the 'Sliver'/'Dive' single, but for the Peel session the band decided to play covers, in effect paying tribute to musical heroes they felt were particularly undersung. Among those heroes, especially for Cobain, were those 'Are We Not Men?' spud-boys from Akron, Ohio, Devo.

Devo began as much an art project as a band. Kent State University students Mark Mothersbaugh and Jerry Casale had an interest in using film and music to explore the dehumanizing, de-personalizing effects of technology, and when each recruited a brother to join them, and drummer Alan Myers was secured, the courageously odd group was born. Even playing in the smallest clubs of Akron and Cleveland, Devo embraced a grand sort of anti-showmanship, using back-screen projections, costumes, puppets and assorted props to enliven such tunes as 'Mechanical Man', 'Mongoloid' and 'Jocko Homo'. Triumphant shows at New York's CBGBs furthered the Devo buzz, and after the release of their Brian Eno-produced 1978 debut album *Q: Are We Not Men? A: We Are Devo*, and a pivotal appearance on *Saturday Night Live*, the band was an electro-avant-garde force to be reckoned with. While the band's second album, 1979's *Duty Now For the Future*, contained some of their strongest material, and their third album, 1980's *Freedom of Choice*, garnered them a pop hit with 'Whip It', the band's recorded output gradually began to take a slow slide toward inconsequence.

The early work remained massively influential, however, and one youngster duly influenced was Cobain. For a kid who sometimes claimed to be gay just to try to separate himself from the dim bullies he saw around him, Devo represented an amazing rock n' roll alternative – here were five guys who were proudly smart, emphatically geeky, not the least bit macho and playing music that not only rocked in its own twitchy way, but also managed with those twitches to enrage typical rocker/stoner dudes.

As Devo-man Jerry Casale told *Trouser Press* in an early band interview:

"All we're doing is reporting the facts... De-evolution is basically an extended joke that was as valid an explanation of anything as the Bible is, a mythology for people to believe in. We're just attacking ideas that people have that they're at the center of the Universe... If there's anything important about history, it's that stupidity wins."

It's not hard to imagine a lot of appeal there for the young Cobain. Years later, the Devo song he and the band decided to do for Peel had little trouble fitting thematically into the Nirvana songbook. In 'Turnaround', the singer is an enraged observer of humankind, who spends the song commanding the listeners to step outside themselves and apply some much needed critical self-evaluation, at which point said listeners will undoubtedly realize what dreadful failures they are. The song was originally released by Devo as one of their singles for the Stiff label and was a part of the band's 1978 'Be Stiff' EP.

The gentle, playful sound
of the Vaselines – Eugene
Kelly and Frances McKee
– was a great inspiration
to Kurt Cobain.

molly's lips

this song was also recorded at the October 1990 Peel session. As Cobain was often quick to point out in interviews, he did not consider himself the first or the best at crafting music that pumped pop songs with rock power. The Beatles were an influence he proudly claimed. Another influence that was equally important to him, although much less well-known to the public at large, was the Vaselines, a band from Edinburgh, Scotland.

The Vaselines were one of those rare bands who managed to combine thoroughly accomplished song writing skills with an amazingly amateurish approach to instrumental technique and studio-work. (The first time they were ever together in a studio, they recorded their first single.) The engagingly tilted minds behind the Vaselines belonged to delicately voiced Frances McKee and gruffer partner Eugene Kelly, later of Eugenius. The band was not prolific – their entire catalogue was re-issued on a Sub Pop CD in 1992 – but they were significant in that, at a time when the rock of the 1980s was particularly bloated, market-driven and joyless, the Vaselines made music brimming with childlike excitement.

'Molly's Lips' plays as an interesting companion piece to 'Sliver'. The vocals are again coming from a child's point of view, and the youngster has been promised that he'll be taken anywhere as along as he stays clean and as long as he keeps planting those wet kisses on Molly's lips. In both the less rocked-out Vaselines original version and the Nirvana version, the bounce of the tune and the sweetness of the melody make it sound like the child/singer is oblivious to how creepy all those kisses are starting to seem, but the listener gets the point.

An earlier version of 'Molly's Lips', recorded with Chad Channing, was the source of some friction between Nirvana and Sub Pop as band and label parted ways at the beginning of 1991. Nirvana owed the label one more single. Sub Pop's Pavitt and Poneman were hoping for an original tune rather than an obscure cover and Cobain felt that that particular version of 'Molly's Lips' wasn't very good, so neither wanted to release it. But Cobain wasn't about to give up one of the new songs he was bringing to Butch Vig for the *Nevermind* sessions. Sub Pop needed to stick to a release schedule, however, and so 'Molly's Lips' it was, backed with 'Candy' by the Fluid.

The Vaselines reunited to play a concert with Nirvana when the 1990 European tour brought Cobain and company to Edinburgh. In the liner notes to *Incesticide*, Cobain listed this show as one of the most rewarding moments of Nirvana's life in the previous year.

On *Incesticide*, the biggest band in rock was in a position to pay tribute to some undersung heros.

son of a gun

this song was the second Vaselines cover to be included on *Incesticide*, and was the third track drawn from the October 1990 session for John Peel. The song takes one of the hoariest of romantic conceits – that all seems sunny when a lover is present and rainy when they're gone – and turns it into a bubbly bit of winsomeness. Given Cobain's usual lyrical territory, it's rather striking that he could visit the Vaselines material completely without irony – he sounds about as happy as he ever would while singing 'Son of a Gun'.

While Cobain couldn't help but see the world in darker terms when writing his own songs, the happiness and innocence celebrated in the Vaselines's music resonated deeply with him. He discovered the Vaselines through a label created by one of Olympia's most prominent scenesters, Calvin Johnson. Johnson played with Beat Happening and established the K label in the early 1980s in order to put out compilation tapes of his favorite bands. In the mid-80s, K began to put out some very influential vinyl, both through the K imprint and through the International Pop Underground series of 45s. These records made unsung bands from around the globe – from the Melvins to Shonen Knife – available in the United States.

It was Johnson's K releases of the Vaselines material that made such an impression on Cobain – enough of an impression that Cobain duplicated the label's crude crayon-drawn "K" insignia as a tattoo on his arm.

"I really like the K label a lot and I admire what Calvin is doing," he told *Option* magazine just prior to *Nevermind*'s release. "They've exposed me to so much good music, like the Vaselines, who are my favorite band ever. The Vaselines reminded me of how much I really value innocence and children and my youth – of how precious that whole world is. I like to watch little kids. I think they're great."

Cobain was no sentimentalist, but he found the childish innocence of the Vaselines music to be deeply affecting.

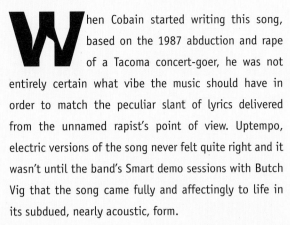

When Cobain started writing this song, based on the 1987 abduction and rape of a Tacoma concert-goer, he was not entirely certain what vibe the music should have in order to match the peculiar slant of lyrics delivered from the unnamed rapist's point of view. Uptempo, electric versions of the song never felt quite right and it wasn't until the band's Smart demo sessions with Butch Vig that the song came fully and affectingly to life in its subdued, nearly acoustic, form.

An electric version of 'Polly' had been partly recorded, and scuttled, during the 'Blew' EP sessions with Steve Fisk. Once the band had hit upon the preferred way of delivering the song at Smart studios, electric versions became something of a joke, hence the tongue in cheek 'New Wave' added to the song's title. The *Incesticide* version of 'Polly' came from the same 1991 BBC session for Mark Goodier that also yielded 'Been A Son'. Aside from the speedy tempo and heavier guitars, lyrically the song is virtually identical to the version that appears on *Nevermind*.

(new wave) polly

beeswax

Pop craftsman and punk defiler – the punk side of Cobain won out on songs like 'Beeswax'.

having made the jump from Sub Pop to David Geffen's DGC label in April 1991, Cobain and the band undoubtedly felt that their punk credentials were somewhat in question. One way of shoring up their underground status while *Nevermind* started to come together was to make an old, ugly screamer like 'Beeswax' available. The song was first released in August 1991 as part of the Kill Rock Stars label compilation. The song dated back to the Dale Crover-drummed/Jack Endino-produced Reciprocal sessions of January 1988. The compilation, which also featured the Melvins and Bikini Kill, was assembled by

musician and one-time Cobain neighbor Slim Moon. It effectively launched the Kill Rock Stars label, which would continue to put out the work of Bikini Kill, featuring Cobain's ex-girlfriend Tobi Vail and his friend, Kathleen Hanna.

In early Nirvana days, Cobain could frequently be spotted in a Scratch Acid t-shirt and 'Beeswax', perhaps more than any other tune, reflects the influence that group had on him. The song's off-kilter rhythms and hard, sloppy guitar back up an especially ragged-throated Cobain as he lets loose an incensed stream of lysergic non-sequiturs.

Discovering his early punk influences, such as Scratch Acid and Big Black, was a major revelation. Cobain once explained, "The intensity, the aggression, the hatred. You could hear a lead singer just scream at the top of his lungs. I felt that way. I wanted to die. I wanted to kill. I wanted to smash things."

the 'Downer' featured on *Incesticide* is the same track that was included on *Bleach* when that album was re-issued by Sub Pop on CD in April 1992. ('Big Cheese' was also included as a bonus.) The song was recorded when the band cut its first official studio demo with Jack Endino at Reciprocal studios in Seattle on January 23, 1988. The band had just let go of drummers Dave Foster and Aaron Burckhard and had recruited former and future Melvins drummer Dale Crover to do the recording with them. The song was one of Cobain's earliest efforts and first appeared on his pre-Nirvana, pre-Novoselic Fecal Matter cassette.

The song is basically an angry denouncement of what's wrong with the world, and also an angered insistence that the singer, at all costs, wishes not to fit in with every or any crowd that might have him. Cobain explained the snarling, sneering misfit tone of early compositions such as 'Downer' by making reference to his troubled early teens.

"I started getting in trouble, vandalizing, rebelling," he told the *Los Angeles Times*. "I was never a bad kid... I was just disgusted, and at that age, I couldn't figure out why. The school counselor would tell me, 'Try to fit in with people, dress the way they do, attend the dances, get into sports.' That was always the big thing – get into sports and your life is perfect."

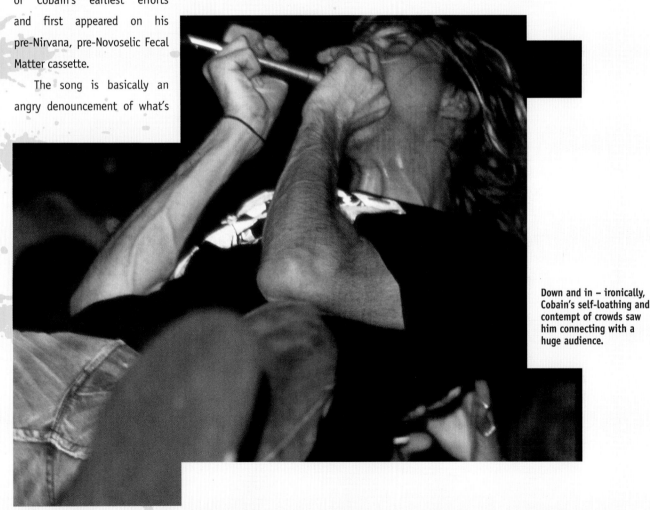

Down and in – ironically, Cobain's self-loathing and contempt of crowds saw him connecting with a huge audience.

downer

mexican seafood

this under-two-minute listing of physical discomfitures was a staple of early Nirvana set lists and was recorded at the Reciprocal session with Dale Crover and Jack Endino. It was first released in November 1989 as a track on C/Z records *Teriyaki Asthma, Vol. 1.*, which also included tracks from L7, which featured future Dave Grohl-girlfriend and Courtney Love-pal Jennifer Finch on bass, and Babes in Toyland, who were fronted by ex-Love bandmate Kat Bjelland.

As short and quick as it is, 'Mexican Seafood' is an interesting study in the split musical personality that turned up in Cobain's early song writing. The song's verses are built along a charging, grinding guitar rhythm and feature punk-worthy lyrics that presage *In Utero*'s fascination with the various seepages that the human body is capable of – here Cobain wails about infections, piss and itchy flakes. But the chorus is built on a few shining chords that, though they back a lyrical complaint about pain during urination, are pop-beautiful. Adding to the split delivery is an unmistakably "Big Rock" break toward the end of the song, in which Cobain reels off one of his few recorded moments of standard rock n' roll boogie-guitar. The title isn't directly related to the tune's complaints, but certainly does conjure-up images of either intestinal distress or, more demeaningly and probably more to the point, an ugly, regretted sexual encounter.

Producer Endino, in a 1992 interview with the *Rocket*, Seattle's alternative weekly newspaper, explained how the birth of the "grunge" sound followed his work on early sessions such as the one at Reciprocal with Nirvana.

"I had a pretty good notion of how to record a grungy, sloppy guitar, because that's the kind of guitar I played myself. I realized early on that I had a terrible guitar sound and how was I going to record it? Then I ended up recording about a hundred bands that had equally terrible guitar sounds, and a new aesthetic was born. What sounded horrible back then is now standard."

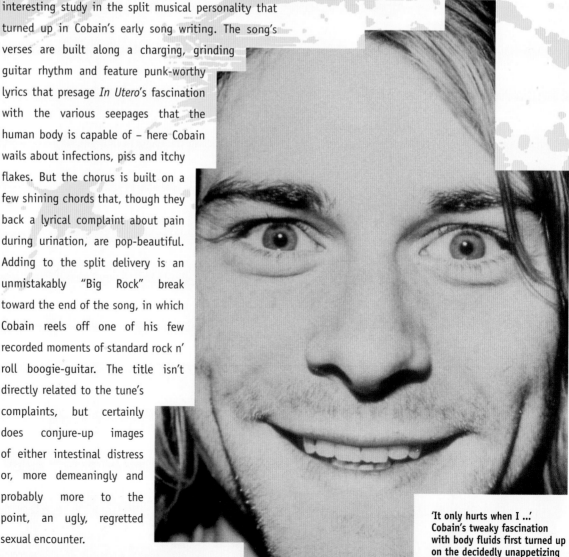

'It only hurts when I ...'
Cobain's tweaky fascination with body fluids first turned up on the decidedly unappetizing 'Mexican Seafood'.

Rock bottom – Novoselic honed his craft on Sabbath and Led Zep before a punk conversion.

this song was also taken from the first Reciprocal sessions and was an integral part of early club shows. The Cobain song was written when both Cobain and Novoselic had undergone punk-rock revelations, and were eager to embrace and replicate some of the sounds that had them so excited. Both players spoke of the seminal, Leeds-born, leftward-looking, art-punk band Gang of Four as a major influence on their early music. With its droopy signature bass line, crisp beat and cleanly chiseled chunks of dissonant guitar, it's clear that 'Hairspray Queen', was the result of a period of Gang of Four immersion. Cobain twists the Gang's sound by delivering the vocals in a strangled voice that is more reminiscent of Scratch Acid's David Yow than it is of Gang of Four's Jon King.

Lyrically, Cobain set to declaring his allegiances punkward, basically using the song to announce that he is an enemy of the creature of the title. That creature's name was actually a handy way of describing the dim-witted, hair-conscious glam-metal rockers of the mid-to-late 1980s whom Nirvana despised. While Cobain and Novoselic had an unabashed love of classic rock, they had some particularly strong feelings of ill will toward what heavy metal had become in the age of Guns n'

Roses and Mötley Crüe. (Metal fans were equally contemptuous of young punks like Nirvana.) *Nevermind* would go a long way toward erasing boundaries of taste – by the mid-90s, definitions of what was punk, grunge, metal or simply rock were pretty interchangeable and useless. But in 1987 there was some very real tension between warring tastes – those perceived to be punk might well be jumped and beaten if spotted around a "rock" club, and the same could happen to a longhaired rocker spotted by punks.

This tension delighted Cobain early on in the band's career. He described one of their earliest gigs, a house party, as a kind of punk vs. redneck-rocker showdown (one in which the band avoided a pummelling by acting louder and crazier than their "enemies").

"These rednecks didn't like us at all. They were scared of us. We were really drunk, so we started making spectacles of ourselves, playing off the bad vibes we were giving the rednecks...Chris jumped through a window and then we played Flipper's 'Sex Bomb' for about an hour. Our girlfriends were hanging on us and grabbing our legs and doing a mock-lesbian scene. That started freaking out the rednecks...That was the idea of punk rock in the first place – to abuse your audience. What better audience to have than a redneck audience?"

"Punk rock kind of galvanized people in Aberdeen," Novoselic explained in an early interview. "It brought us together and we got our own little scene after a while. Everybody realized – all the misfits realized – that rednecks weren't just dicks, they were total dicks. And punk rock had this cool political, personal message. You know what I mean? It was a lot more cerebral than just stupid cock rock."

hairspray queen

aero zeppelin

From the beginning, Nirvana played even its simplest riffs with wild punk abandon.

between recording with Dale Crover at that first Reciprocal session and finding Chad Channing as a permanent-for-a-while bandmember, Cobain and Novoselic ran an advert in Seattle's *Rocket* that read as follows: "Heavy, light punk rock band: Aerosmith, Led Zeppelin, Black Sabbath, Black Flag, Scratch Acid, Butthole Surfers. Seeks drummer." That list of influences demonstrates the mix of old-time rock grandiosity and jagged new-punk rage the band was trying to mix up in its early days. Cobain took on the issue of making that mix as a lyrical theme in this song, recorded at the Reciprocal sessions.

'Aero Zeppelin' was a standard tune in early club appearances, sometimes showing up on set lists along with a bona fide cover of Led Zeppelin's 'Immigrant Song'. While the song's deadly earnest riffing doesn't give any indication of the Cobain pop hooks and melodies that would come shortly, the lyrics are a fairly insightful examination of the relationship between young fans and rock heroes past their prime.

'Aero Zeppelin' represents a lesson Cobain and Novoselic picked up from mentor Buzz Osborne of the Melvins – that old-school rock could be made fresh again if it was reworked and revitalized with fierce intensity, as opposed to simply being reheated and restaged for the sake of posturing like a rock star. The Melvins had begun as a jam band playing Led Zeppelin and Black Sabbath covers to the red-eyed delight of stoners in Aberdeen and Bellingham, and Osborne made the jump toward creating his own wildly innovative dirge-metal without forsaking what he loved best about the old rock n' roll. With this song, Cobain and Novoselic were attempting to make the same jump.

"Buzz was the punk rock guru of Aberdeen," Novoselic said in a 1992 interview. "He's the guy who spread the good news around town but to only the most deserving, because a lot of people in Aberdeen would discount it. I tried to turn people on to it, but they'd be like...one guy I know, I remember, he goes, 'Ah that punk rock stuff, all it is is "Want to fuck my Mom! Want to fuck my Mom!"' And then I listened to Generic Flipper and it was a revelation. It was art. It was valid. It was beautiful. 'Cause I gave things validity like 'Is it as good as *Physical Graffiti*?' And it was suddenly, like 'Sure it is – if not better'."

Walk this way – Nirvana took their early rock n' roll influences and twisted them into something entirely new.

big long now

this track was recorded by Jack Endino, originally for inclusion on *Bleach*, and it's another of the band's explorations into the super slow, super big sound of the Melvins. Buzz Osborne had led the Melvins from being a premier cover band to one of the Northwest's fastest hardcore bands, but ended up settling in to become one of the slowest bands that anybody had ever heard. Funereal rhythms, tectonically slow guitar riffs, and vocals of alternately whispered fears and harshly screamed rage – that was the basic formula for Melvins tunes such as those that appeared on the highly influential 1987 album *Gluey Porch Treatments*. And that is principally the formula Cobain and Novoselic followed in grinding out 'Big Long Now', (whose quite inscrutable lyrics seem to be centered on post-coital unease).

In a 1992 interview, Cobain recalled an early, formative Melvins show:

"They started playing punk rock and had a free concert right behind Thriftways supermarket, where Buzz worked, and they plugged into the city power supply and played punk rock for about 50 redneck kids. When I saw them play, it just blew me away. I was instantly a punk rocker. I abandoned all my friends, because they didn't like any of the music. Then I asked Buzz to make me that compilation of punk-rock songs and got a spike haircut."

"Yeah, I infected Kurt and Krist," Osborne bragged to Lorraine Ali in a 1993 *Option* interview. And despite the decidedly non-Melvins-ish turn Nirvana's music took on *Nevermind*, Osborne remained proud of his punk inheritors. "The reason *Nevermind* sold a lot is because it's a good record," he said.

Reciprocal-era Nirvana bandmate and current Melvins drummer Dale Crover concurred. "Some people said *Bleach* was such a better record than *Nevermind*. I don't agree. I think *Nevermind* makes *Bleach* sound like a shit record."

aneurysm

incesticide closed out with a tune recorded during the BBC session for Mark Goodier at the end of 1991. Though a slight song by Nirvana standards, 'Aneurysm' is interesting in that it shows the band at play. Cobain is bending a few simple lyrics around to make fun of pop conventions and drug-use rituals ("shoot the shit", "beat me out of me"). The song is also one of Nirvana's only songs to make use of a sudden, major style shift – a minute in and the tune jumps from *Bleach*-like riffing to highly-glossed, harmony sweetened "Big Pop." Lastly, the song is interesting as an early, especially potent clue that Dave Grohl's phenomenal drumming was going to make the band a heavy contender in the mainstream rock world.

A slightly more pumped up version of 'Aneurysm' was recorded in January 1991 by Nirvana-soundman Craig Montgomery and appeared as part of a joint B-side with 'Drain You' and 'Even In His Youth' when DGC released a 'Teen Spirit' CD single in 1991. The Montgomery version of 'Aneurysm', with the *Incesticide* versions of 'Turnaround', 'Son of a Gun' and 'Molly's Lips', along with 'D-7' and 'Even In His Youth', made up a 1991 EP titled 'Hormoaning'. This was released in Australia and Japan as a promotional EP in conjunction with Nirvana's tour there in early 1992.

Clinical humor – from the start. Cobain's lyrics explored the shadowy realms of drugs, disease, depression and insanity.

With their second major-label effort, Cobain and Nirvana created a great, raw, self-lacerating rip of an album. They also a created an album that didn't have any trouble selling – upon its release in September 1993, it debuted on the pop charts at number one. But it wasn't an entirely easy or pleasant undertaking. *Nevermind* had hit the pop world as a wonderfully invigorating surprise from an unknown Seattle band. The making of *In Utero* took place under a media microscope, and the album was turned into an ugly, distorted tabloid scandal before a note of music had even been heard by the public.

"We've been wanting to record a really raw album for almost a year now, and it looks like we are finally ready to do it," Cobain told Robert Hilburn of the *Los Angeles Times* in a September 1992 interview. In February 1993, the band headed to Pachyderm Studios outside Minneapolis, Minnesota, to work with producer Steve Albini.

Cobain always counted on a creative rapport with a producer to fully realize the band's sound. He'd been happy to have Jack Endino there as the band recorded *Bleach* and Butch Vig for *Nevermind* (though he did subsequently make some disparaging remarks about each producer). With Albini, Cobain was excited at the prospect of working with someone who would not only understand the nuanced clamor Kurt was looking for, but who was, in fact, a respected musical influence. Albini had been a pivotal figure in the early 1980s Chicago scene, when he fronted Big Black. Their abrasive, industrial-strength, discontented sound was

widely imitated and appropriated, not least of all by early Nirvana. Following the demise of Big Black, Albini had assembled Rapeman, which featured the rhythm section from another of Nirvana's punk idols, Scratch Acid. While continuing to perform and record for himself, Albini had become best known as a producer (though, for reasons of principle, he has always taken the credit "recorded by" rather than "produced by"). Albini had worked on records by such underground notables as the Pixies, Helmet, the Jesus Lizard and P.J. Harvey.

Starting at the end of February, the band and Albini set to work – without interference from management or record company – and stayed true to a punk-rock ethos and recording pace. The band was recorded playing live as a group, with only vocals and occasional guitar parts added as overdubs. There was no reliance on studio trickery – Albini achieved his starkly vibrant trademark sound entirely through mike placement and recording levels. Within two weeks the album was recorded and mixed and everyone seemed happy.

"Dealing with the members of Nirvana was entirely pleasant for me," Albini said at the time of the album's release. "I have no hard feelings whatsoever about the process of making the record, and I would consider Dave Grohl a personal friend. The modus of making this record was pretty honorable. I was working with a great three-piece rock band, and they banged out some of the best music they're capable of over a two-week period. The stupid stuff started happening after the band and I parted company in February."

"Stupid stuff" was a fitting term for what ensued when Geffen execs and Nirvana management couldn't disguise their disappointment with the tracks the band

in utero

In the raw - with *In Utero*, Nirvana created a great, back-to-basics album, but it wasn't easy getting there.

had turned in. Suddenly, the biggest band of the 1990s was being told that their music wasn't good enough to be released. Things got stupider when some major media outlets got wind of that disappointment and turned it into a pop melodrama, pitting Albini, Geffen and Nirvana against each other in a three-way war of words and spin management. Nirvana at first were adamant about releasing the record exactly as they had recorded it, but under unrelenting pressure from the record company, and conscious that the press was by and large enjoying their uncomfortable position, the band began to reconsider. "People aside from myself and the band managed to turn the making of *In Utero* into a very ugly bit of emotional warfare," Albini said. "And the standard of journalism brought to bear on this Nirvana project was shoddy and embarrassing."

Finally, when angry self-confidence gave way to exhaustion and resignation, the band made some concessions toward giving the album a "friendlier" sound. Producer Scott Litt, well-known for his work with

Nirvana answered the polish of Nevermind with a fierce, raging shot of prime punk. In Utero showcased a great band playing at its furious best, and a sharp song writer at his most agitated.

REM, re-mixed 'Heart-Shaped Box', and 'All Apologies', and all the tracks were re-mastered to bring out bass parts and accentuate the vocals. Albini was decidedly unhappy with the released version of the record. "Somebody was frightened that this excellent record might not be perfect," he said. "So they chose to master it into a mundane record." Cobain began making nasty comments about the quality of Albini's original work. Amid all the bad blood and ill will, *In Utero* was released on September 21, 1993, and debuted at number one on the pop charts.

The songs on *In Utero* mostly came from a period of writing that Cobain undertook in the spring of 1992, when the band had long stretches of inactivity. Cobain was living in a Hollywood apartment on North Spaulding Street with new wife and mother-to-be Courtney Love. This was, ironically, one of Cobain's periods of heaviest drug use, but – confounding all the junkie stereotypes – it was also a time in which he remained capable of producing some of his finest work. However, like the creation of the album itself, the creation of the songs was not without crisis. When the Cobains returned home from Nirvana's tour of Europe in July, they discovered that burst pipes in a bathroom had destroyed precious notebooks that were full of poems and song ideas that Kurt had been working on. Soon afterward, the couple moved to a house in the Hollywood Hills and Cobain simply started over with a fresh pile of notebooks.

In true punk fashion, Cobain wanted to follow up the multi-platinum success of *Nevermind* with a sick joke – the working title of *In Utero* was *I Hate Myself and Want to Die*. How literally did he mean that?

"As literal as a joke can be," he told David Fricke of *Rolling Stone*. "Nothing more than a joke. And that had a bit to do with why we decided to take it off. We knew people wouldn't get it; they'd take it too seriously. It was totally satirical, making fun of ourselves. I'm thought of as this pissy, complaining, freaked-out schizophrenic who wants to kill himself all the time. 'He isn't satisfied with anything.' And I thought it was a funny title. I wanted it to be a title of the album for a long time. But I knew the majority of

the people wouldn't understand it."

With Albini, the band recorded a track with that title that ended up in a rather improbable spot – as the opening track on the first album celebrating MTV's charmingly nightmarish pre-teen pop-critics Beavis and Butt-head (*The Beavis and Butt-head Experience*). Cobain enjoyed that irony. "Yeah, you know, there were a lot of Beavises and Butt-heads back there [in Aberdeen]. The only difference is they weren't as clever as the guys on TV."

A second working title was also a joke, but more at the band's own expense – Cobain wanted to mock his own pop-formulae by calling the album *Verse Chorus Verse*. The band also recorded a song with that title, which ended up on the 1993 compilation album *No Alternative*. Cobain finally returned to his fascination with babies, embryos and female reproductive organs with *In Utero*. He followed through on that title with the artwork he helped design for the record. The front picture was one of his favorite "visible woman" anatomical models, the back was a pastiche of uterine and fetal medical models accented with orchids and umbilical cords.

The Cobain-designed artwork of *In Utero* – a winged humanoid with visible internal organs – made it to the concert stage in mannequin form.

Serve the servants

The big, dumb, music industry question surrounding the release of *In Utero* was – "Can these guys give us another 'Teen Spirit'?" Cobain took the question head on in the first line of the first song when he groaned that teenage angst had paid off well for him, followed with the confession that since the pay-off, he has simply grown bored and old. Clearly, this album would not be a work of "teen spirit", which in point of fact, had been a spirit greatly misunderstood to begin with. Some considered the lyric petulant or grossly cynical, but mostly it was a product of Cobain's darker sense of humor. *Nevermind* had been attacked by some "old" Nirvana fans as being a crass marketing move – a punk sell-out. What better, more unsettling response could Cobain offer than to simply cop the plea?

For all the fuss and bother about the making of *In Utero* – the nervous whispers that the band had created an album of hideous, unlistenable noise – the records kicks off with an energizing, satisfying blast. Far from sounding like some outré-punk experiment, 'Serve the Servants' is one of the most rock n' roll tracks Nirvana ever recorded. Straddling a slow, steady riff that would do Neil Young's Crazy Horse proud, Cobain, sounding thoughtful and archly restrained, offers some keen reflections on his band's rise to pop dominance.

As Nirvana-mania had kicked into high gear, Cobain had been the most reluctant of superstars, deeply bothered by the way his songs immediately lost all shadings of meaning as they became mass-market product. In the band's downtime during early 1992, when most of *In Utero*'s songs were written, Cobain and Courtney Love were occasionally amused by the absurdity of Nirvana as an object of pop culture – Kurt at times pranced around their apartment to high-volume playbacks of neo-chanteuse Tori Amos's overwrought cover version of 'Smells Like Teen Spirit'. But that August's *Vanity Fair*, in which Love was depicted so unfavorably, proved that media attention could not only turn nasty, but also bring about horrible personal difficulties. The article brought out some self-admitted homicidal impulses in Cobain, but in 'Serve the Servants' he affected a more ironically detached view of the critics, the fans and himself.

Cobain also worked in a gibe at "self-appointed judges" – basically all those people who felt free to take pot-shots at him and the band without ever considering what it might be like to put themselves on the line in any way. Though Cobain grew weary of the media spotlight and feigned disinterest in what was said about him, he was in actuality nearly obsessed with following coverage of himself. Instead of being the blasé punk, Cobain was still, at heart, the small-town kid who couldn't believe his name was in the big-city papers.

"I'd try to get Kurt to stop reading stuff about himself," Courtney Love told *Rolling Stone* in a 1994 interview. "I wouldn't buy him magazines anymore. But he'd sneak off and buy them. He got addicted. Every gibe, every caricature, every reference. This was someone who couldn't deal with being paraphrased wrongly. So to be the cultural reference for every fucking thing there was...and this was someone who had been pretty much unnoticed most of his life. He wanted to be popular, very much a people pleaser."

To protest the press treatment Love had received, Cobain used some witch-hunt imagery (as he would also in 'Frances Farmer Will Have Her Revenge On Seattle'). A line in the first verse refers to the medieval practice of public dunkings, by which a woman suspected of witchcraft would be tested. Because witches were said to be made of wood, it was believed that they would float at the surface of the water – a non-witch would simply sink. It was, much like the ordeal of being put on trial by the modern media, a serious no-win situation.

In the most personal lines of the song, Cobain sings of a painful childhood in which he wanted a father, "but instead I had a dad." These lines are followed by a direct address to Kurt's father, Don Cobain, in which the song says "I don't hate you anymore." As the verse might indicate, Cobain's relationship hadn't been as much troubled as it was non-existent. He had lived with his father's new family after his parents' divorce and had felt miserably out of place. Once he moved out, father and son became, for all intents and purposes, strangers. Don did follow news of his son's career and, after seven years of estrangement, initiated contact with Kurt by showing up at a benefit that the band played in Seattle. The two had a short, cordial conversation and Don met Courtney and Frances Bean. Don never saw his son again.

In a 1994 interview, David Fricke asked Kurt Cobain if the "father" lines in 'Serve the Servants' reflected some worry that Kurt himself might not be cut out for fatherhood.

The young Cobain family in happier times. Kurt's reconciliation with his father would be made through the lyrics of 'Serve the Servants'.

"No, I'm not worried about that at all," Cobain said. "My father and I are completely different people. I know I'm capable of showing a lot more affection than my dad was... I would never allow [Courtney and myself] to be in a situation where there are bad vibes between us in front of [Frances]. That kind of stuff can screw up a kid, but the reason those things happen is that the parents are not very bright."

While the song expressed scorn for those Cobain felt had been judging him, he also played down the whole notion that those judges would be attracted to some mystique about him in the first place. "The legendary divorce is such a bore," he sighed in the chorus, obviously tired of having his childhood plumbed for deep meaning.

scentless apprentice

as story after story of Kurt Cobain's travails with heroin were kicked around in the press, an unfortunate image began to take shape – that he was a disengaged, unfeeling, dumb junkie who happened to be able to write some songs and play guitar. It all made for good tabloid copy and stand-up comic material, but it was not accurate. Cobain was undoubtedly a tormented soul and quite a few of those torments were self-inflicted, but his worth as an artist, thinker and musician was much broader than the "junkie-with-guitar" stereotype allowed.

Cobain was not a voracious reader, but he was a

Literary debts: 'Scentless Apprentice' was drawn from a novel. William S. Burroughs received 'Special Thanks' on *In Utero* for being a cherished inspiration to Cobain.

devoted one. Writers Katherine Dunn, Susan Faludi and William S. Burroughs all received "Special Thanks" in the *In Utero* credits, and 'Scentless Apprentice' took its theme from the 1986 novel *Perfume*, by the German writer Patrick Süskind.

The novel, set in eighteenth-century France, tells the peculiar story of a bastard infant who is born with two startling characteristics – he has an amazingly developed sense of smell, which he uses to assess the world around him, plus he gives off absolutely no odor of any kind from his own body. He is thought to be devil-spawn by the nurses who reluctantly care for him at his orphanage but is eventually apprenticed to a master perfume maker. His natural abilities make him an extraordinary talent in the field of fragrances, but his darker impulses begin to emerge. While the smells of most humans and human activities disgust him, occasionally he will find a woman whose scent is so beguiling that he feels compelled to kill her – to own her scent as it were. He is eventually put on trial for his crimes but, in a rather phantasmagorical closing sequence, manages to manipulate a rabid mob into having an orgy rather than an execution.

Cobain hadn't intended to turn his reading of the novel into a song, but a need for strong lyrics arose under some musically surprising circumstances – for the first time, the band collaborated from square one in writing a song. The piece started with a basic guitar riff that Dave Grohl had come up with. Cobain didn't think the riff sounded all that promising – in fact he felt it was a little too reminiscent of the Sub Pop-era grunge sound the band wanted to distance itself from. But as Kurt, Krist and Dave jammed around the riff, it turned into something more impressive. Kurt came up with a guitar line of ascending notes that pulled against the basic riff, Krist arranged a second section the song could move to, and a fierce, group-penned composition was born. It was the one *In Utero* track on which all three band members received a song writing credit.

The sound was fierce enough, in fact, that Cobain reached back to the disturbing tale of *Perfume* for his

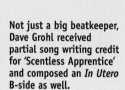

Not just a big beatkeeper, Dave Grohl received partial song writing credit for 'Scentless Apprentice' and composed an *In Utero* B-side as well.

lyrics. His vocals, snarled out like a supremely pissed-off W.C. Fields, basically sketch out the ideas of Süskind's story. His desperately screamed "Go away's" are particularly chilling and, in light of the book, seem to cut two ways – it's either what the singer/apprentice hears from those who hate him, or it's what the singer/apprentice screams at those he hates. The angry strength of 'Scentless Apprentice' demonstrates how well-connected the trio could be, and how quickly they could come up with potent music when those connections were working.

The 'Scentless Apprentice' guitar riff wasn't Dave Grohl's only song writing contribution during the *In Utero* sessions. A Grohl-penned and sung tune, 'Marigold', was recorded and used as a B-side for the 'Heart-Shaped Box' single. Much of the song writing Grohl was doing during this period later turned up as material on the 1995 debut Foo Fighters album.

heart-shaped box

Kurt Cobain and Courtney Love began to take a serious interest in each other while Nirvana was in Los Angeles in May and June 1991, working on their sessions for *Nevermind*. Dave Grohl served as something of a go-between for the two at first – he knew Courtney through mutual friend Jennifer Finch of L7. In order to make her romantic intentions clear to Kurt, Courtney passed a gift to him by way of Dave: a small heart-shaped box filled with trinkets and a tiny doll. Heart-shaped boxes subsequently became collectables around the Cobain-Love household – there were shelves of them at the Hollywood homes the couple shared through most of 1992.

Much of the song writing for *In Utero* was done in these apartments during Nirvana's long stretches of down-time during that year. Their first apartment, on North Spaulding Street, had a large walk-in closet that often served as a song writing sanctuary for Kurt, and that's where 'Heart-Shaped Box' was written. In fact, if Cobain hadn't immediately been so fond of what he was playing, the track may have ended up being a song for Courtney Love's band, Hole. "The only time I asked him for a riff for one of my songs, he was in the closet," she told *Rolling Stone* in a 1994 interview. "We had this huge closet, and I heard him working on 'Heart-Shaped Box'. He did that in five minutes. Knock, knock, knock. 'What?' 'Do you need that riff?' 'Fuck you!' Slam. He was trying to be so sneaky. I could hear that one from downstairs."

Kurt continued to work on the song, but found that when he introduced it to the band, it strayed away from the delicate vibe he was after and turned into a big, noisy jam. Shortly before the *In Utero* sessions, Cobain was ready to give up on what would become the album's signature tune, but let the band have one last crack at it. Suddenly, it came together. Cobain discovered the coolly restrained vocal style of the song's verses, Krist came up with the demonic loping bass line that powers the chorus (one of Cobain's favorite bits of Krist-work), and the whole band gave the tune the dynamic shape it needed. 'Heart-Shaped Box' became a keeper.

Cobain told several interviewers that the song was inspired by seeing documentaries and news features on terminally ill children. The song's alternate moments of gentle sadness and angry sarcasm may be emotionally true to those real-life situations. But Cobain also seemed to be taking a look at his relationship with Courtney. Much as he described the symbiotic connection between the two babies in 'Drain You', Cobain's connection to his wife isn't illuminated with standard romantic couplets – instead there's talk of cancer, umbilical cords and "meat-eating orchids." (Cobain said he liked orchids because they reminded him of vaginas. There are orchids scattered among the medical models of embryos and uteruses in the artwork Cobain designed for the back of *In Utero*.) The song's most piercing line of lyric showed again some of Cobain's very self-aware, self-deprecating humor: "I got a new complaint."

Cobain spoke of his relationship with Love in a November 1993 interview with Gavin Edwards in *Details* magazine.

"Everyone thinks of me as this sad little spineless puppy who needs to be taken care of. It sickens me. When I first met Courtney, I thought of her as this totally independent, self-serving person and I really respected her for that – that's why I fell in love with her. Since we've been married, I've found that she's a bit more insecure. I'm glad – it's nice to know she isn't going to take off one day. I didn't think I'd ever have a best friend, let alone a mate."

'Heart-Shaped Box' was one of the two tracks that were re-mixed by long-time REM producer Scott Litt after the band finished work with Steve Albini. It was with Litt, in May 1993 and at Bad Animals Studios in Seattle, that Cobain added some acoustic guitar and the dreamy-to-razor-sharp harmonies that helped make the song a standout. The song took on yet another form when it became the basis for a wondrously heady video directed by Anton Corbijn.

In the June 1995 issue of *Musician*, Krist Novoselic spoke out against pending music censorship bills that were working their way through a number of state legislatures. To make his point, he used a line of 'Heart-Shaped Box' to show the folly of turning words and lyrics into criminal acts.

"One of the lines is 'Broken hymen of your highness.' In that song, the word 'hymen' is used as a metaphor. In the context of these censorship bills, if you were to discuss the hymen as a normal, natural part of the female anatomy with a teenager, you would technically be breaking the law."

It was through L7's Jennifer Finch, foreground, that Kurt Cobain met Courtney Love during the making of *Nevermind*. The first heart-shaped box was exchanged shortly thereafter.

The rock n' roll family – Courtney, Kurt and Frances Bean.

rape me

'Rape Me' was one Cobain tune that shifted thematic focus between the time it was written and the time it was recorded. When the band was in Los Angeles in June 1991, in a rest period during the mixing sessions of *Nevermind*, Cobain picked up an acoustic guitar and began toying with the chords of 'Smells Like Teen Spirit' and the theme of 'Polly'. He came up with 'Rape Me'. In some ways the song was indeed intended as "Polly's" response to the man brutalizing her – it's also a promise to him that vengeance will some day be hers.

"Basically, I was trying to write a song that supported women and dealt with the issue of rape," Cobain told Rolling Stone. "Over the last few years, people have had such a hard time understanding what our message is, what we're trying to convey, that I just decided to be as bold as possible. How hard should I stamp this point? How big should I make the letters? It's not a pretty image. But a woman who is being raped, who is infuriated with the situation...it's like 'Go ahead, rape me, just go for it, because you're going to get it. I'm a firm believer in karma, and that motherfucker is going to get what he deserves, eventually...So rape me, do it, get it over with. Because you're going to get it worse'."

By the time it was recorded during the *In Utero* sessions, the song had become more self-reflexive and the rape had become figurative. Cobain doesn't seem to be singing for any "Polly" – he's singing as Cobain. Tired and hurt from the struggle to maintain integrity and privacy, the singer gives himself up – resignedly offering himself to the smiling fans and hungry media who have ceased thinking of the object of their attentions as anything human. Cobain makes it clear he's singing for himself – and the band – in the song's second section, where he takes an "inside source" to task for spreading falsehoods.

In Cobain tradition, the singer packs a punch that is both powerful and ambiguous with the song's key line "I'm not the only one." The singer may be telling us he's not the only one getting hurt by a harsh spotlight – he's got a family too. But perhaps he wonders why he's the one of the three Nirvana members to be singled out for special attention. Or, he may simply be announcing to his nemeses that there are other "stars" who deserve equal torment.

The song brought a couple of controversies upon the band. They were forbidden from playing it in their performance at the September 1992 MTV Video Music Awards. The band complied, playing instead a version of 'Lithium', but not before Cobain drove some MTV flunkies close to apoplexy by strumming the opening bars of 'Rape Me'. The song was also thought to be the real reason why the huge K-Mart and Wal-Mart chains of discount stores refused to stock *In Utero*. (The administrators from each company at first said they hadn't ordered the number-one record in the country because there was little consumer interest.) The album became acceptable to the retailers when a special printing of the album's artwork was arranged and 'Rape Me' was listed, in rather ingenious disguise, as 'Waif Me'.

Something shocking – the band couldn't play 'Rape Me' at the 1992 MTV Video Awards, but managed to raise a few eyebrows backstage.

francis farmer will have her revenge on seattle

For the artists, actors and musicians of Seattle, the story of Frances Farmer's life has remained a disturbing cautionary tale of the crushing, authoritarian forces a free-thinking artistic mind can come up against. Born in 1914, Farmer was a drama student at the University of Washington in Seattle, and in the mid-1930s gained some local fame as one of the theater scene's budding stars. The future looked bright for Farmer, with the New York stage and Hollywood films beckoning. But controversy that would hound her the rest of her life began when, as a college student, she wrote an anti-religious essay for a leftist magazine and won a trip to Moscow. She survived the bad press that the incident provoked, eventually making it to New York. She did well in some Broadway productions and went on to success in Hollywood. Between 1936 and 1942, Farmer appeared or starred in 14 films, including *Come and Get It*, *Flowing Gold*, *Among the Living*, and *Son of Fury*.

Unfortunately, the pace of her work took its toll on her and she was further broken by the dehumanizing Hollywood star machine. She began to drink heavily and, after several drunk-and-disorderly arrests, was committed – by her mother – to a mental institution. Rather than help her, the institution depressed and unhinged her even further – she was very likely driven insane by the conditions under which she was forced to live. Upon her release, she did battle with her alcoholism and addiction to pain killers and sedatives, which she'd picked up as a "patient." She could not resume her career, and many in the press continued to gloat that her sorry state was just punishment for her heretical political beliefs. Her mother, along with a string of unsympathetic judges, continued to find reasons to have her re-committed to a series of institutions and mental hospitals. She later claimed that she had been raped almost every night she was confined.

Legend has it that Farmer was lobotomized during one of her final hospital stays, but in 1958 she became active in show business again, with parts in a movie (*The Party Crashers*), a play and a long-running soap opera on a local television station in Indianapolis. She died in 1970, and her autobiography, *Will There Ever Be A Morning?* was published in 1972.

The specter of a beautiful, fragile woman driven to degradation and an untimely death by a hateful society couldn't help but have appeal to Cobain, who empathized strongly with Farmer's story. In his song, Cobain doesn't retell that story, so much as take on her voice to mock the witch-hunters who had undone her. He also predicts a kind of Frances-led apocalypse, in which the actress will return as flames to "burn all the liars". For Farmer, all the things that were supposed to bring her happiness – career, fame, money – brought destruction instead. When Cobain reflects on his so-called success, he winds up concluding that he misses the simple comfort of being sad.

For all the supposed "punkiness" that *In Utero* was supposed to spit at its listeners, the lengthy title 'Frances Farmer Will Have Her Revenge On Seattle' stands out as decisively anti-punk. Cobain was bothered by the growing tendency among "alternative" and neo-punk bands to give their songs ostensibly ironic, one-word titles.

Cobain wasn't the first Seattle musician to pay tribute to Farmer. During the 1970s and 1980s, several punk shows were held on the University of Washington campus in the Group Theatre – which had been named after the New York theater company that Farmer was a part of. In the last month of his life, Cobain attempted to contact William Arnold, the author of what's considered the definitive biography of Farmer. Arnold intended to respond, but Cobain was dead before the writer had a chance.

Beautiful, talented, delicate, and crushed by an unsympathetic world. The plight of actress Frances Farmer was an intensely moving story to Cobain.

Young, stupid, and in love – Cobain twisted some clichés of romance in his own love song of sorts, 'Dumb'.

dumb

this sweet Beatle-inflected song gives the lie to the supposed storm that swirled around the making of *In Utero*. This gentle, soothingly melodic whisper of a song was recorded with supposed sonic-madman Albini at the recording console, and made it on to the album without any extra post-production sweetening. Albini also apparently allowed his ogreish personality to recede long enough to record a cello – Kera Schaley's mournful lines add to the track's delicate atmosphere.

Cobain wrote the song in the summer of 1990, when, particularly inspired by the anti-testosterone pop of the Raincoats and the Vaselines, he began to follow through on some of his own poppier instincts. 'Sliver' was one result, and a basic version of 'Dumb' was another. In April of that year, Cobain had finally become satisfied with 'Polly' during the Smart demo sessions – he brought the song to life by singing it softly and strumming it on an acoustic guitar. It was while toying with the 'Polly' chords that Cobain discovered the 'Dumb' melody. For a lyrical theme, he decided to step into pop territory as well – this is simply a song about being happy. Of course, because it's a Cobain song, happiness has shadows – the singer can't decide if he has found contentment or simply lacks intelligence. Cobain first debuted the song for the person who had been responsible for his discovery of the Vaselines – Calvin Johnson of K Records. In the autumn of 1990, Cobain played the song for a radio show hosted by Johnson on Olympia's KAOS.

Cobain was impressed enough with what the Vaselines could do with lovey-dovey sentiments on a song like 'Son of a Gun' that he covered it. He creates the same kind of love-among-the-pastel-colors feel in the middle section of 'Dumb', but the sweet sentiments take on an edge when one realizes that Cobain is plaintively singing about inhaling glue with the object of his affections so that the couple can enjoy a common hangover.

'Dumb' seems a good example of something Cobain told Gavin Edwards just as the record was being released: that he did not – as had been rumored – wish to drive fans of *Nevermind* away from the band with *In Utero*. "Let's face it, we already sold out two and a half years ago. There's no sense in trying to redeem yourself by putting out an abrasive album and pretending you're a punk rocker."

In Utero had been said to be unlistenable – but 'Dumb' was one of the sweetest things Cobain had ever written.

93

Not part of America's team – Cobain took another shot at mass machismo with 'Very Ape'.

though it has power and a distinctive snarl, 'Very Ape' was something of a throwaway tune on *In Utero* and probably represents what the people at Geffen were afraid of when they first heard the *In Utero* tracks. While a quick collaborative effort worked to the band's benefit on 'Scentless Apprentice', a quick Cobain effort here yielded one of the album's slimmer efforts. Cobain had the music in mind before he had lyrics and so for a while 'Very Ape' had the working title 'Perky New Wave Number'. By the time it was recorded, it sounded more like a heavy-metal tune. In some ways, the tune's simple lyrics are a follow up on *Bleach*'s 'Mr. Moustache' – the song is basically an impassioned denunciation of machismo.

'Very Ape' is, however, a little more nuanced than 'Mr. Moustache'. While the *Bleach* tune had been written partly as a rip at the beefy thugs Cobain had dealt with in Aberdeen, by the time Cobain wrote the *In Utero* tunes, he had become accustomed to a different type of brute, an odd creature of the rock n' roll world – the macho poseur. The character in 'Very Ape' is acting big and tough and hoping no one discovers that he is entirely naive – he's trying to prove his masculinity through hipness.

That character is, however, a little fuzzy around the edges. Cobain's use of the first-person in 'Mr. Moustache', or 'Lithium', was pretty clearly him singing in character. But throughout 'Very Ape' – especially when the singer takes pride in being "the king of illiterature" – it's not entirely clear where Kurt leaves off and where the 'Very Ape' character begins.

very ape

milk it

This is another track that mainstream fans of *Nevermind* probably expected when they heard from Geffen execs that *In Utero* was abrasively unlistenable. Loud, noisy, ugly, unpleasant – 'Milk It' is all that and more. It's also a bracing, thoroughly invigorating tune. And it even has some melody.

Though he presented himself as an iconoclast, Cobain had always allowed his song writing to be shaped for the marketplace. Much of his original pre-Sub Pop work with Nirvana was a little too arty and noisy for the label, so the band streamlined its sound and became purveyors of grunge. Signing with Geffen had in many ways freed Cobain to pursue his pop impulses but, in fact, some of the lightest, poppiest song ideas that he had wanted to develop for *Nevermind* were rejected by people at the record company – they could sell loud guitars to the public, but knew there wasn't much of a market for Vaselines-style whimsy. By the time he was crafting music for *In Utero*, Cobain thought he and the band had finally been musically liberated. He was a song writer with millions of records sold, after all, and had earned the right to freely follow his muse. As the ensuing stink over *In Utero* proved, Cobain wasn't as free as he thought. But 'Milk It' points in the direction that he may have taken the band if Nirvana had continued to record.

The power of the song lies in the formidable, razor-sharp arrangement. Lyrically, 'Milk It' was another quickie job for Cobain – it is basically 'Drain You' come to full fruition. Throughout *In Utero* – from its songs to its artwork – Cobain took his fascination with disease and anatomy to artistic extremes, and with 'Milk It' he wrote a love song that expresses its devotion scatologically. Milk, shit, viruses and parasites all become shrieked terms of endearment. The song also contains the terribly prophetic line "Look on the bright side is suicide."

In the superlative Nirvana biography *Come As You Are* Cobain told Michael Azerrad that 'Milk It' provided a hint of things to come. Cobain pointed out that he was working to get past what he saw as a Nirvana song-writing formula, and that future music might sound closer to 'Milk It' than to some of *In Utero*'s catchier tracks.

"I definitely don't want to write more songs like 'Pennyroyal Tea' and 'Rape Me'. That kind of classic rock and roll verse-chorus-verse mid-tempo pop song is getting real boring. I want to do more new wave, avant-garde stuff with a lot of dynamics – stops and breaks and maybe even some samples of weird noises and things – not samples of instruments. I want to turn into the Butthole Surfers basically."

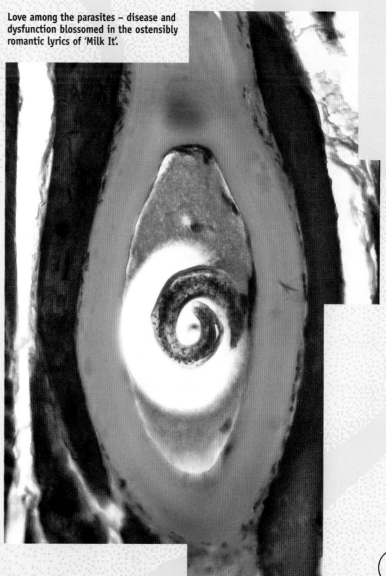

Love among the parasites – disease and dysfunction blossomed in the ostensibly romantic lyrics of 'Milk It'.

pennyroyal tea

this is the *In Utero* song with the longest history. It was written, and first recorded, when Kurt Cobain and Dave Grohl were living together in Olympia during the winter of 1990. Cobain had moved into Tracy Marander's house on North Pear Street as their relationship became more serious, but when they split up, she was the one to leave. In October of that year Dave Grohl became Nirvana's drummer, and at first lived with Krist and Shelli Novoselic, but soon moved in to share Cobain's house. By several accounts, the combined sloppiness of Grohl and Cobain worked to turn that residence into a breath-takingly filthy mess – but occasionally enough clutter was cleared so that the two could set up a four-track recorder and work on material. 'Pennyroyal Tea' was the very quick, inspired result of one of these four-track sessions. Cobain didn't think the song was strong enough for *Nevermind*, and left it undeveloped. When it was revived for *In Utero* it became a standout track.

Though the song sounds like it is another in the line of Cobain's soft-loud-soft, verse-chorus-verse pop constructions, it was one of the first of his songs to establish that formula. Perhaps that's why Cobain didn't seemed entirely thrilled with the song by the time *In Utero* was released – he had become disenchanted with his own song writing process.

"I guess I start with the verse and then go into the chorus," he said in a 1994 interview. "But I'm getting so tired of that formula. And it is formula. And there's not much you can do with it. We've mastered that – for our band. We're all growing pretty tired of it. It is a dynamic style. But I'm only using two of the dynamics. There's a lot more I could be using. Krist, Dave and I have been working on this formula – this thing of going from quiet to loud – for so long that it's literally becoming boring for us.

It's like 'OK – I have this riff. I'll play it quiet, without a distortion box, while I'm singing the verse, and now let's turn on the distortion box and hit the drums harder'."

Given all the medical references in *In Utero*, and the anatomical artwork that bedecked the cover, the title and lyrics of 'Pennyroyal Tea' are particularly appropriate. Pennyroyal is a flowering mint plant that has long been used in European and American folk medicines. The plant's oil can be used as an effective mosquito repellent, but also turns up in herbal remedies of questionable efficacy. Pennyroyal tea is believed to work as an abortifacient, but its record of success is shaky – chemical agents in the tea may possibly cause uterine contractions, but only when it is consumed in nearly lethal quantities. That was an appealing contradiction to Cobain, who had been exposed to – and developed a contempt for – the herbalism, homeopathy and varied hippie-folkie alternative medicines of the sandal-wearing, New-Age segment of Olympia's bohemian population.

At the time Cobain wrote 'Pennyroyal Tea', he was in the process of a break-up with Tobi Vail, and had become disillusioned with Sub Pop, the Olympia scene and his own prospects of finding artistic fulfillment. The song is basically sung by someone who is hoping for a complete purge of his problems – in effect, he wants to abort himself (or, in the case of the third verse's reference to laxatives – excrete himself). A reference to "cherry-flavored antacids" has some personal resonance – Cobain was troubled throughout most of his life by a mostly untreatable stomach disorder that had him in chronic pain. The lyrics are also notable for an unusual musical reference. If Cobain's pennyroyal-induced "self-abortion" is successful, he says he hopes for an after-life befitting that of Canada's transcendental, world-weary poet, novelist and song writer, Leonard Cohen.

in utero

Anemic royalty – despite internal friction, Nirvana was still capable of greatness on *In Utero*, as evidenced by standout tracks such as 'Pennyroyal Tea'.

Radio friendly unit shifters – for all the stress, strain and craziness surrounding them, Nirvana had both a number one album and an artistic triumph with *In Utero*.

radio friendly unit shifter

necessarily want that, but I've finally admitted that we're in the entertainment business."

Still, he got a dig in at *Nevermind* and "Nirvana-mania" with the title of this track, which appropriates the crass, reductionist, bottom-line thinking of a record company marketing department. The song is another of *In Utero*'s "scary" tracks – there's nothing radio-friendly about it. Against an insistent bass riff, a bashing drum rhythm and piles of guitar noise, Cobain asks "What is wrong with me?" and offers a few cleverly turned phrases and random thoughts on the price of success.

Cobain elaborated on being such a tremendously successful "unit shifter" in another 1993 interview, explaining that selling millions of records and bringing on a pop trend could still leave an empty feeling.

"Sometimes you wonder if anything has changed. Just because everyone starts wearing flannel shirts doesn't mean they think about the world any differently. If we had changed things, you'd hear a lot better music on the radio, wouldn't you? I can't deal with all that...the future of grunge in America and all that. All I can do is worry about our band...and keep from becoming another rock n' roll cartoon."

Cobain hated the notion of being a mass-marketed "voice of a generation."

after *Nevermind*'s release, Cobain's opinion of the record tended to flip-flop. As the album grew from an unexpected hit to a major pop-culture signpost, Cobain grew less and less comfortable with the music and attempted to distance himself from it. He would sometimes shrug off the sonic quality of *Nevermind*, saying that to him it didn't sound any better than a Mötley Crüe record, or that the bunch of songs weren't any more important than anything Cheap Trick had ever put together. But eventually he came to feel that it wasn't necessarily shameful to create something that was so popular.

Just before *In Utero*'s release, he told *Details* magazine, "I always hated when bands like Poison would say, 'We just want to give these hard-working blue-collar people an escape for a couple of hours.' We don't

Uncontrollable urges – arrangements for tracks such as 'Tourette's' were quickly hammered together in the studio.

tourette's

in Utero was made very quickly. Cobain said shortly after the sessions. "All the basic tracks were done within a week. And I did 80 percent of the vocals in one day, in about seven hours. I just happened to be on a roll. It was a good day for me, and I just kept going."

'Tourette's' was one of the final, and fastest-assembled, songs on In Utero, and was recorded when Cobain could afford to blow his throat out with some manic shrieking. The song basically filled the space that 'Territorial Pissings' took on Nevermind. It begins with a brief Novoselic vocal appearance (intoning "Moderate Rock" in his best oily FM DJ voice) and then kicks into a simple, fierce, over-the-top punk workout. The song takes its title from a neurological disorder named after the French physician who first diagnosed it. With Tourette's syndrome, an afflicted person is prone to involuntary tics and uncontrollable verbalization, which often takes the form of either shouted obscenities or repetition of what is being spoken to the person. "Cufk," "Tish," and "Sips" were the only three words listed on In Utero's lyric sheet for this one, though Cobain seems to be screaming words a little more excretory in nature. Some listeners felt this track was pure filler, but there was certainly some dark humor in Cobain's suggestion that he – the idolized, platinum-selling "prophet of grunge" – might simply be someone whose bad brain made him yelp dirty words.

Some felt he was an unfit father, but Cobain spoke openly of the deep and powerful love he had for daughter Frances Bean.

all apologies

in Utero's final track, and the second of the two re-mixed by Scott Litt, is a tender and gracefully melodic statement of humility from Cobain. It was written at Cobain and Love's Hollywood apartment on North Spaulding, in the spring of 1992 – a time when Cobain was not getting along well with his band mates, his record company, his management or his public. In Utero opened with the angry, cynical self-defense of 'Serve the Servants' but closed with the acutely self-aware 'All Apologies'. Cobain lets the listener know he sees himself in as harsh a light as anyone else does, and recognizes his limitations. The songs ends with the cryptic affirmation "All in all is all we are." Nirvana debuted it at the 1992 Reading Festival, with a dedication from Kurt to Courtney and 12-day-old Frances Bean.

The lyrics include some witty plays on words, as well as a revised version of one of Cobain's favorite graffitos. He had once delighted in spraying "God is Gay" on the walls of various establishments around Aberdeen. Now, in a sweet, resigned voice, he sang "Everyone is gay." Not a bold statement from someone who could mix milk and shit in a love song perhaps, but still a fairly brave line from a major rock figure speaking to a mass audience. He took another ground-breaking, gender-twisting step for a straight rock n' roller shortly after In Utero's release, when he granted an extensive interview for and appeared on the cover of the February 1993 Advocate, a magazine whose readership was mostly gay men. The subject of gender roles and sexual preference came up again when

Cobain sat for an August 1993 Los Angeles Times interview wearing one of his favorite thrift store dresses: "Wearing a dress shows I can be as feminine as I want. I'm heterosexual...big deal. But if I was a homosexual, it wouldn't matter either... I respect people who promote the way that they feel sexually."

Aside from provoking some gender discussion and making the mea culpas of the title, 'All Apologies' stood out as one final uplifting example of what was possibly Cobain's greatest talents – he could write beautiful songs.

"I don't want to see 'Cobain is God' spray-painted on the wall," Cobain said upon In Utero's release. "My ego is already inflated way past the exploding stage. I feel embarrassed saying this, but I'd like to be recognized more as a song writer. I don't pay attention to polls and charts, but I thumb through them once in a while and see, like, Eddie Vedder is nominated number-one song writer in some magazine, and I'm not even listed."

The wave goodbye – the band didn't know it, but In Utero would be their final studio album.

unplugged in new york

With amps powered down and acoustic guitars in hand, Nirvana delivered a performance that let the power and beauty of Cobain's songs shine through in surprising ways.

in Utero was a *de facto* live album – it presented Nirvana in raw, loud, un-sweetened form – and was a moving document of a great band flexing its formidable musical muscles. That record was followed up with a bona fide live album, recorded when Nirvana decided to take part in MTV's *Unplugged* series.

Unplugged had started as a fairly novel idea – bands could turn down their amps, put away their effects units and let their song writing shine. By the time Nirvana recorded their session, on November 18, 1993, the series had become somewhat tired and overdone – rather than offering a revealing glimpse of musicians working in an intimate setting, it was more often a precious, somewhat self-congratulatory run-through of hits played quietly. Surprisingly, Nirvana's set did manage to restore the power of revelation to the series. Alternately ragged and brilliant, the acoustic versions of Cobain tunes, along with some well-chosen covers, seemed to loom larger the more quietly they were played. For a band whose reputation had been built with loud, charged records and instrument-smashing concerts – a band whose success some attributed to the crafty use of volume knobs and distortion pedals – Nirvana offered something of a shock when they played a set softly: underneath all that grunge, all that distortion and all that teen spirit – there had always been wonderful songs.

Following the release of *In Utero* in September, Nirvana prepared for a major tour of the US and Europe – what would be its final tour. As the band had in the past, it made a point of lining up opening bands that the band members particularly appreciated and wanted to promote – the Meat Puppets, the Breeders, the Boredoms, Half Japanese, Come, Shonen Knife and the Butthole Surfers would all share bills with Nirvana throughout the band's 45-date swing through the US. During some intensive rehearsals prior to the tour, Nirvana also made a line-up change – for the first time since the departure of Jason Everman, they became a foursome again. The added member was guitarist Pat Smear (née Ruthensmear) of the infamous LA punk band the Germs.

"For the longest time, we had looked for a

For the *In Utero* tour, Nirvana became a foursome again, adding guitarist Pat Smear, right.

second guitar player in Nirvana," Dave Grohl told Chris Mundy in a 1995 *Rolling Stone* interview. "We thought it would be great to get Steve Turner from Mudhoney, or Buzz [Osborne] from the Melvins or Eugene [Kelly] from Eugenius. We were rehearsing one day, and Kurt came in and said 'Pat Smear from the Germs is going to be our second guitar player.' Krist and I had never met him, and I just imagined this bloated, tattooed, bitter old mess. And he came to rehearsal and it was so incredibly refreshing that it made everything instantly great."

The Germs, fronted by the self-destructive Darby Crash, turned out to be a remarkably influential band in punk and hard-core circles but they were little-heard during their brief existence. They were one of the wildest and most innovative groups in a punk scene that flourished in LA during the late 1970s, which also included the likes of Black Flag, the Circle Jerks and X. The band's recorded legacy centers on their one studio album, 1979's *GI* on the Slash label, which was produced by Joan Jett. Songs like 'Lexicon Devil' and 'Manimal' are vital precursors to much of what the rock underground would produce in the 1980s. The Germs achieved their greatest degree of notoriety when their exhilaratingly shambolic performances became the centerpiece of Penelope Spheeris's punk documentary *The Decline and Fall of Western Civilization*. But by the time of the film's release, in 1980, Crash was dead of a heroin overdose.

Smear went on to record a pair of solo albums for SST, and became part of a duo called Death Folk. He supported himself largely through extra work in films and television. (He appeared in Prince's 'Raspberry Beret' video!) At the time he was summoned for an audition with Nirvana, he was working behind the counter at the SST Superstore on the Sunset Strip in Hollywood.

Some cynical observers saw the recruitment of Smear as another Nirvana attempt at resuscitating their punk credibility, given the debacle that their involvement with Steve Albini had turned into. But the move was largely pragmatic – Cobain benefited greatly in live performances when he had a second guitar backing him up. And Smear himself certainly felt there

was nothing calculated about his addition to the line-up. Shortly after joining the band, he told Joe Gore in *Guitar Player*, "It's all very natural, honest and true to what they're really about. I've rehearsed with them, I've watched them write songs, and there's nothing contrived about anything they do."

Though Cobain, Novoselic and Grohl were very aware of the Germs' legacy, Smear wasn't very familiar with Nirvana's work. Still, Smear's mix of raw feel, solid chops and spirited persona turned out to be a great fit in the band. "I'd heard their album maybe once. But everything felt really natural right away, because what they do is very similar to what I've always done."

With Smear on board, the band brought along one other musician on tour – cellist Lori Goldston of Seattle's Black Cat Orchestra re-created the somber lines that Kera Schaley had added to 'Dumb' and 'All Apologies' on *In Utero*. The tour kicked off on October 18, with a headlining set at the Arizona State Fair in Phoenix. As the band worked its way eastward and through the Midwest, the shows were generally energized and exciting. Nirvana demonstrated their talent on stages decorated with creepy trees and winged mannequins that were similar to the translucent woman on the cover of *In Utero*. They played raucous, generous sets and Cobain finally seemed to enjoy – or at least tolerate – engaging the crowd in the band's performance.

Mid-tour, on November 18, while the band was in New York City, Nirvana taped its *Unplugged* concert at Sony Studios. On a small stage bedecked with candles and a forest of orchids (Kurt's favorite flower), Kurt, Krist and Pat hunched on stools and strummed acoustic guitars while Dave Grohl tapped at his drums with brushes. The mood was hushed, and there was little interaction with the appreciative crowd, but the performance wasn't without a few flashes of Cobain's famously cutting, self-deprecating humor ("I guarantee you I'll screw this song up," he muttered before a David Bowie cover song). Even so, watching Cobain make music in so humble a setting made him a warmer, more inviting figure than many would have suspected after the tales of star fits and junkie-dom that continued to circulate.

Nirvana's *Unplugged* session succeeded in that it

was an enlightening behind-the-hype view of a very capable, talented band. That the archangels of grunge could play music of such stunning subtlety was a surprising treat for fans, and the subdued readings of what had been high-volume missives proved to be a minor epiphany – it turned out that Nirvana's secret weapon all along had not been its rage, its attack or its volume – but its songs.

The *Unplugged* performance was recorded with the expectation that it would be an interesting sidelight to the long, strong career of a world-class rock band. But, sadly, it became something closer to a eulogy when it was released in October 1994.

Kurt Cobain never stopped growing as an artist, but he also never figured out a way to make peace with his personal demons. By the time Nirvana left for a European tour in February 1994, Cobain was in decent spirits and had apparently got his heroin addiction under control, but his health was in an ever-fragile state. There were a few powerful performances in Europe, but on March 1 in Munich, Cobain lost his voice halfway through a show and was advised by doctors there that he was suffering from exhaustion and needed several weeks of rest. Remaining concert dates were postponed, and Cobain and Courtney Love settled into a hotel room in Rome. On the morning of March 4, Love found Kurt in a coma – he'd written her a suicide note and proceeded to wash down 50 sedatives with champagne. He was rushed to a hospital and was revived after five hours of treatment.

Back in Seattle, Cobain's behavior became increasingly erratic, and he again resumed a heavy heroin habit. At the end of March, Love arranged for an "intervention" – an orchestrated confrontation with Cobain in which several of those who loved him and worked closely with him (including Novoselic, Grohl, management and record company people and some close friends) encouraged him to get some professional help. Cobain agreed to spend time in a Los Angeles-area rehabilitation center, and headed to LA on March 30 – after purchasing a shotgun and dropping it off at his Lake Washington home. He spent a day at the Exodus Treatment Center, but on April 1 ran away from the grounds and made his way to the airport, where he caught a flight back to Seattle.

Love hired private detectives to track Cobain down, and his mother, Wendy O'Connor, filed a missing person report with the Seattle police. But Cobain would not be found until it was too late to help him. On Tuesday, April 5, in a room above the garage of his Lake Washington home, Kurt Cobain wrote a long suicide note, gave himself an injection of heroin, and then ended his life with a shotgun blast to the head. He was 27 years old.

Too soon gone – a troubled Cobain saw suicide as his only escape route.

The gentle, mournful rendition of 'About A Girl' that follows is right on the mark. In fact, although the ostensible purpose of *Unplugged* was for musicians to reinterpret their songs in an acoustic mode, this version sounds like a reinvention – it sounds more genuine than the original. Whereas 'About A Girl' was the one *Bleach* track to hint at Cobain's budding pop-sense, here the song shines as a fully realized pop lament. While the *Bleach* version's electric power gave the tune the lope of a Smithereens tune, here the song's Beatle-esque heart is exposed for all to see – the song could easily be a *Help*-era out-take.

Given the elevated status the *Unplugged* album took on after Cobain's death, 'About A Girl' makes for a great opening track – it's a reminder that Cobain the song writer was a fine craftsman even back in the unabashedly grungy days. And it's also a reminder that no matter what the prevailing trends around him were, and independent of the advice of labels and management, Cobain's music led him to take chances.

"Even to have put 'About A Girl' on *Bleach*, was a risk," Cobain told David Fricke shortly after the *Unplugged* session. "I was heavily into pop, I really liked REM, and I was into all kinds of old '60s stuff. But there was a lot of pressure within that social scene, the underground – like the kind of thing you get in high school. And, to put a jangly REM-type of pop song on a grunge record, in that scene, was risky."

The pop appeal of 'About A Girl' – when all around was grunge – had shown Cobain's more likely influences, such as pop songsmith Michael Stipe of REM.

the *Unplugged* sessions kick off with some warm applause, to which Cobain responded with a rather formal "Good Evening". Then he announces this song from *Bleach* by saying, "This is off our first record. Most people don't own it".

about a girl

come as you are

Nirvana played several songs from *Nevermind*, but avoided reinterpreting any of the major grunge anthems from that album ('Teen Spirit', 'In Bloom', 'Lithium', etc.). Instead, they focused on songs that had already had a gentler dynamic in album form, and 'Come As You Are' – whose odd, watery sound had made it stand apart on *Nevermind* to begin with – was a choice that benefited greatly from an acoustic presentation. (Acoustic – but amplified. Since its creation, *Unplugged* has been a misnomer, as every act appearing has, in fact, plugged in to electric amplification. That being the case, Cobain used a chorus effect pedal to recreate that same odd, watery guitar sound from the album.)

In its tougher, album form, 'Come As You Are', had sounded like an invitation, but also a challenge. Cobain was, in effect, throwing down the gauntlet and announcing that he would not judge those he was addressing if they would simply present themselves without affectation. In its *Unplugged* version, the song seems to become a much more open, friendlier invitation, and perhaps even a request of a favor – two years of celebrityhood and its attendant scrutiny has given Cobain no choice but to "come as he is" and he's wondering if his audience might be willing to join him. In the midst of all the craziness going on in Nirvana's world, Cobain's heartfelt delivery of the song's sentiments becomes tender, even touching.

Because the *Unplugged* album was released months after Cobain's death, it had the eerie effect of presenting a performer who was singing to his fans from beyond the grave. In that light, 'Come As You Are' was a particularly difficult track to listen to – it was hard not to get a creepy feeling from hearing an impassioned Cobain sing out – as if he were trying to convince himself – "I swear to you I don't have a gun."

A gentle invitation – 'Come As You Are' and many other *Unplugged* tracks picked up fresh nuance in their subdued form.

jesus doesn't want me for a sunbeam

Cobain's love of, and promotion of, Scottish band the Vaselines had remained undimmed since he had first discovered their music through Calvin Johnson's K Records while living in Olympia. Notwithstanding the band's slim output, Cobain continued to talk them up in interviews, and made a point of staying in contact with half the Vaseline brain trust – Eugene Kelly. Kelly had gone on to form Eugenius, a band that rocked harder and more straightforwardly than the Vaselines, and for which he continued to write some masterfully poppy songs. Eugenius recorded two albums, and it was their recording and touring plans that quickly took Eugene Kelly out of the running when he was briefly considered as Nirvana's second guitarist.

Throughout Nirvana's career, Cobain took the opportunity to reflect some of his limelight toward a few of rock n' roll's most eccentric and under-sung heroes. If the bands were still around and up to the task, they might be asked to open a show for Nirvana. Otherwise, they would be lauded with kind words from Cobain and a conspicuous appearance on one of his t-shirts. Greg Sage and the Wipers, the Raincoats and Daniel Johnston were a few of those who benefited from Cobain's desire to share the attention he received, and the Vaselines may have received the best plugs of all. Two Vaselines covers were on *Incesticide*, this one made it to *Unplugged* and it was partly Cobain's unflagging support of the band that got Sub Pop to collect and re-issue the band's entire catalogue on a CD in 1992 (*The Way of the Vaselines: A Complete History*).

This haunting song, written by Eugene Kelly and Vaseline-partner Frances McKee, is written in the shape and style of an old hymn, and captures the wised-up, semi-bitter sentiments of someone who expects he has no place in heaven. The song gave Nirvana a chance to stretch a bit, musically – Dave Grohl played bass while Krist Novoselic contributed some melancholic accordion lines.

Cobain had great faith in music but little respect for the excesses of organized religion. He echoed a dim view of the notion of heaven in this Vaselines cover.

the inclusion of a David Bowie tune on the *Unplugged* set list was perhaps the performance's biggest surprise – it seemed somewhat out of character for a band that had just made a point of releasing a pointedly punked-out, resolutely un-commercial album to be covering a song by one of rock n' roll's most self-consciously arty, commercially successful superstars. But it brought Cobain full circle back to one of his earliest rock n' roll passions.

Though Cobain had hated everything that the glam-metal scene of the mid-1980s had produced, he had an abiding love for the original glam and glitter-rock of the 1970s. Roxy Music, David Bowie and T-Rex remained as, if not song writing influences, listening pleasures. When Cobain, Novoselic and original drummer Aaron Burckhard made one of their first-ever public appearances, playing a gig at the GESSCO Hall in Olympia back in 1987, they didn't take the stage in punk guise – Cobain was in a floral shirt, platform shoes and some liberally applied eye makeup. He sang in a *faux*-British accent that reminded most in the audience not of Johnny Rotten, but of David Bowie.

'The Man Who Sold The World' was the title track of one of Bowie's earliest albums, released in 1970. (Before he recorded as David Bowie, he had put out a few mod-era novelties under his given name - David Jones.) That album had Bowie's sexually ambiguous, stylishly flamboyant persona coming into its own, and pointed the way toward his next identity – Ziggy Stardust, alien-born rock n' roll frontman. With the showmanship and grand production of later Bowie works, some fans may have forgotten that his earliest work had a guitar-strumming, Dylanesque feel to it. Cobain and Nirvana recaptured that spirit, and reminded the audience that before Mr. Bowie settled into years of bland superstardom, he was a smart, crafty song writer. Cobain sounds quite pleased to be able to pull that off. "I didn't screw it up, did I?" he asks with some genuine wonder at the songs end.

Cobain surprised many fans by turning back to his early glam influences with a David Bowie cover during Nirvana's *Unplugged* performance.

the man who sold the world

111

pennyroyal tea

seemed to tie in with something Krist Novoselic said in a taped message that was played for the thousands of mourning fans who gathered in Seattle at the Flag Pavilion the Sunday after Cobain's suicide:

"We remember Kurt for what he was: caring, generous and sweet. Let's keep his music with us; we'll always have it, forever. Kurt had an ethic toward his fans that was rooted in the

the loose feel of Nirvana's set is clear as they get ready to play this song from the then just-released *In Utero*. Band members aren't sure what song to play next – they're simply following Cobain's lead. *Unplugged*'s most affecting moment came when Cobain decided to do a solo performance of 'Pennyroyal Tea' – it's just him strumming a guitar and singing while the audience, and the rest of Nirvana, listens in. This must have been the way Dave Grohl first heard it as Cobain wrote the song on a four-track recorder in the Olympia apartment they shared back in 1990.

Here was a perfect opportunity to hear how much of the power of Nirvana's music began in Cobain's head. This song, whose successful arrangement on *In Utero* depended on wild dynamic shifts and a pummelling drum beat, hardly seems smaller when strummed softly on an acoustic guitar – the conclusion being that the type of guitar didn't really matter because the most amazing instrument in Nirvana was Cobain's voice.

He doesn't, however, want to be coddled for his successful solo turn. As the song comes to a quiet end, a band member is moved to say, "That sounded good." Cobain's quick, less-than-gracious response: "Shut up."

The song's reference to "anaemic royalty" later

punk-rock way of thinking: no band is special, no player royalty. If you've got a guitar and a lot of soul, just bang something out and mean it. You're the superstar, plugged into tones and rhythms that are uniquely human; music. Heck, use your guitar as a drum; just catch a groove and let it flow out of your heart. That's the level that Kurt spoke to us on, in our hearts. And that's where he and the music will always be, forever."

dumb

'dumb' was a natural choice from *In Utero* for the *Unplugged* set – it hardly changed at all from record to live performance. Lori Goldston's cello adds the intriguingly somber counterpoint to Cobain's gentle assessment of his chances for happiness, while Novoselic's fluid bass lines keep the dreamy song moving forward. Of particular note on this performance, as well as on 'Polly' and several others, is Dave Grohl's clear, sweet background vocals – his abilities as a vocalist, and song writer, would become clear when he released the Foo Fighters debut album in 1995.

Putting on a show – by the time of the 1993 *In Utero* tour, Nirvana had come a long way from the sloppy house parties of just a few years before.

Despite a brutal misappropriation, 'Polly' remained one of Nirvana's most affecting songs – a beautifully rendered glimpse of a moment of horror.

polly

'p

olly' had been a breakthrough song for Cobain – a song so powerful that it required a major shift in band strategy. And it was, in fact, the song that had first taught Nirvana the power of being "unplugged." Cobain's unhappiness with the fast, electric version of the song – what came to be known as '(New Wave) Polly' – led him to get away from Nirvana business as usual. At the Smart Studios demo sessions

he had realized that the problem was not with the song but with the approach. When he turned the amps off and simply strummed the song on acoustic guitar – while singing coolly restrained vocals – the song's strengths became apparent. After the release of *Nevermind*, 'Polly' had been used as something of an "unplugged" moment in Nirvana concerts – the song that allowed for a break in the din and a few moments of more sublime listening.

Here, 'Polly' was largely unchanged from its *Nevermind* version, but its inclusion in the set says something about Cobain's commitment to his work. In the *Incesticide* liner notes, he had railed against a pair of rapists who had committed their crime while singing this song. Other bands had had songs taken hideously out of context before and often responded by retiring the song from performance. But instead of having that incident ruin the song for Cobain, he took it as a challenge to reclaim it. As performed here, 'Polly' was again one of Nirvana's most powerful works.

on a plain

'**O**n a Plain' was perhaps Cobain's greatest triumph of accidental song writing – it was largely a song about not having anything to say in a song. But the lyrics that Cobain had put together from notebook poems and last-minute improvisations during the final day of *Nevermind* sessions had held together and become meaningful in their own obtuse way. And the band clearly enjoyed playing the song enough that it remained a part of their set during the *In Utero* tour and at the *Unplugged* performance.

In its subdued form, 'On A Plain' went a long way toward making any lingering debate on the slick sound of *Nevermind* somewhat pointless. Here the song was without any double-tracked vocals, without any compressed guitar, without any radio-friendly sweetening, and yet it still jumped out as a thoroughly engaging piece of prime pop. In the wake of *Nevermind*, Nirvana had sometimes had to answer to charges of selling out, and were expected to mutter punk oaths about how the "record company made us do it." But at this point they were free to let their Beatles-roots show without apology, and 'On A Plain' sounded as catchy and uplifting as it ever had.

Cobain made one notable, but not all that significant, change in the song's lyrics. In the second verse, instead of opening with "My mother died" as he had on the record, he substituted "My brother died."

something in the way

attaining the chilly vibe of 'Something in the Way' had been one of the most difficult problems of the *Nevermind* session. It didn't come together until an exasperated Cobain collapsed on a couch in the recording control room and strummed an acoustic guitar to show Butch Vig what he wanted – at which point Vig simply recorded him right there and succeeded in capturing the album's moodiest piece. The vibe was easily and effectively recreated for *Unplugged*, with the band's exceptionally light touch, Lori Goldston's gliding cello lines and Cobain's delicate vocal approach coming together to again paint a picture of the life Cobain had lived beneath the North Aberdeen bridge a few years before and a world away.

plateau

the Meat Puppets (from Phoenix, Arizona) are one of the longest-lived and most musically accomplished of the early 1980s indie bands. The band, which includes brothers Curt and Cris Kirkwood and drummer Derek Bostrom, began as a lark in 1982 when the trio decided to mix up hardcore punk raucousness, honky-tonk song writing and decidedly amateurish musical abilities on their self-titled debut album. The band might have been a little-heard, quickly forgotten joke, but they followed their debut up with a couple of post-punk masterpieces: 1983's *Meat Puppets II* and 1985's *Up On The Sun*. On those records, it became clear to many that the Meat Puppets were a serious, double-edged threat – their post-hippie, avant-jazz chops were routinely astonishing, and they were capable of writing remarkably original compositions, full of hummable melodies, moving choruses and lysergically bent lyrical visions.

The band survived into the 1990s, releasing records that usually had many moments of brilliance but had no chance of breaking out into mainstream success. On the strength of their careening, improvisational live shows, they continued to convert unsuspecting concert-goers into die-hard fans, yet were still beloved by a few and unknown to millions. That changed when Cobain began to wear their t-shirts and talk them up in Nirvana interviews. Suddenly, hordes of *Nevermind* fans were discovering the heady pleasures of Meat Puppets albums such as *Huevos* and *Monsters*. The Meat Puppets profile rose even higher when, at Cobain's insistence, they were offered the opening slot on the first part of the autumn 1993 *In Utero* tour. Since that portion of the tour coincided with the plans for the *Unplugged* recording, the Meat Puppets were welcomed along to Sony Studios, where Nirvana did three Puppets cover tunes. In addition, Curt Kirkwood played guitar along with Nirvana on all three covers, while brother Cris played guitar on two songs, bass on one, and contributed some backup vocals.

In a 1995 interview with Mark Kemp for *Option* magazine, Curt Kirkwood tried to express his gratitude to Cobain. "At that fucking point in my life, for Kurt Cobain to come from out of nowhere...I mean, I had no fucking association with the guy, none whatsoever, until – boom! – there he was. When you've been dogged all your life, and all of a sudden some little champion comes through for you... I don't know what to say."

This first Puppets cover is a dusty, country-tinged song about a place. That place – the plateau – is one of natural beauty that has been defiled by human actions. Specifics are hard to pin down because, in typical Meat Puppets fashion, what comes through in the song are free-floating bits of dream logic and nightmarish imagery. Still, the saddened, somewhat forbidding, tone of the song indicates that humans have not acquitted themselves well where the plateau is concerned. Explaining his world view to Kemp, Curt Kirkwood said, "I'm not discounting humanity because I feel like we're scum; it's not a derogatory thing. To me it's just fucking reality." "We're just a little channel for the horrors of the world," added Cris.

oh me

Clearly the vocals didn't get in the way of Cobain's appreciation, and one can hear more easily the power and craft of the Kirkwoods' song writing in Cobain's much sharper vocal deliveries of these early songs. Cobain occasionally had trouble taking pleasure in his own work – or, more accurately, in the reactions to his own work. But on *Unplugged*, particularly on the Meat Puppet covers, one can hear that Cobain still found joy in getting inside a song and bringing it to life. During a 1994 interview with David Fricke for *Rolling Stone*, Courtney Love spoke of Kurt's faith in making music: "He never really put that down. That was the one area that he wouldn't touch like that. I got to sit and listen to this man serenade me. He told me the Meat Puppets second record was great. I couldn't stand it. Then he played it to me – in his voice, his cadence, his timing. And I realized he was right."

'Oh Me' is built on a starkly beautiful melody, and seems to be a tender, though somewhat foggy, celebration of new fatherhood. "Our lives were so fucked up," Curt Kirkwood recalled of the year that *Meat Puppets II* was written and recorded. "We were into all kinds of weird shit. We were so young. A lot of stuff on that album has to do with having kids."

the Meat Puppets had recorded nine albums by the time they were teamed up with Nirvana on the road in 1993. But the album that had remained a significant personal favorite for Cobain was their second, titled appropriately enough, *Meat Puppets II*. On their debut, the band had begun recording at hardcore speeds, with plenty of attendant noise. On the second album, they slowed things down considerably and allowed for less clutter – thus revealing some formidable song writing talent. Even on that more melodic album though, one of the things that made the Meat Puppets hard to listen to, for some, was the vocals of the Kirkwood brothers – drifting, lazily off-key, full of hit-and-miss harmonies – they were very much an acquired taste.

Arizona's redoubtable Meat Puppets got some international spotlight when Kurt Cobain became their "little champion."

lake of fire

'Lake of Fire' is probably the most Meat Puppet-ish of the three Meat Puppets songs covered here. With a bouncy, country feel, the song lays out the Kirkwoods' vision of Hell. Curt

A goofy sense of humor sometimes masked the formidable song writing talents and instrumental prowess of the Meat Puppets.

Kirkwood provides some devilishly slinky lead guitar, and Cobain clearly relishes digging into the lyrics – he adds some extra grit and twang to his bemused vocals. When the song ends, Cobain keeps the twang on for a "Thank you kindly," and makes a point of introducing the Meat Puppets to the crowd. Interestingly enough, around the time the Meat Puppets helped to record Nirvana's cover of this song for *Unplugged*, they were about to release their own cover – a new Meat Puppets version of 'Lake of Fire' turned up on 1994's excellent *Too High to Die*.

In the 1995 interview with Mark Kemp, Curt Kirkwood clearly still had some conflicted feelings about having been "discovered" by Cobain and, consequently, Nirvana fans. The Meat Puppets had been paying their punk/underground dues longer than almost any other band, and Kirkwood seemed to find it troubling that after all their hard work, the commercial success of the Meat Puppets was due to a simple nod of approval from Cobain. "They chose to have us come along with them, but I wrote those songs. I don't know why things happen. I have thought a lot about it – why? why? – but I don't know."

But getting the break from Cobain and Nirvana obviously meant a lot to Kirkwood and his band, and it was a cruel twist for them to lose their "little champion" so soon after getting to know him. Curt Kirkwood worked out some of his feelings toward Cobain with a song on the Meat Puppets' 1995 album *No Joke*. Borrowing a piece of lyric from 'About A Girl', the song was called 'For Free'.

"It's just a fucking disclaimer, basically," Kirkwood said at the time of the album's release. "The title says it all. ...I didn't take Cobain to be some kind of huge icon. To me he was just a person I worked with. That's a rarity for me, because one of my icons is work. And when you spend time working with somebody like him – well, that shit's fucking cool, man. It's totally real."

Apologies regretfully accepted – Nirvana fans gathered during a Seattle memorial service for Cobain, April 10, 1994.

With its final, soothing mantra changing from the recorded version's "All in all" to "All alone is all we are," perhaps no song – following Cobain's death – took on as poignant a cast as this one did. The song began to sound like an extension of the suicide note he had left, in which he had addressed Nirvana's fans directly:

"I haven't felt the excitement of listening to as well as creating music, along with really writing something, for two years now. I feel guilty beyond words about these things...Sometimes I feel as if I should have punched a time clock before I walk out on stage. I've tried everything within my power to appreciate it, and I do. God, believe me, I do. But it's not enough. I appreciate the fact that I and we have affected and entertained a lot of people. I must be one of those narcissists who only appreciate things when they're alone. I'm too sensitive..."

In that note, Cobain ended with a line of lyric from Neil Young's 1979 album *Rust Never Sleeps*: "It's better to burn out than to fade away." Young had never met Cobain, but was an admirer of his talents, and was moved to dedicate an album to him – 1994's *Sleeps With Angels*. He talked about Cobain with Eric Weisbard in a September 1995 *Spin* interview:

"I really could hear his music. There's not that many absolutely real performers. In that sense, he was a gem. He was bothered by the fact that he would end up following schedules, have to go on when he didn't feel like it, and be faking, and that would be very hard for him because of his commitment. The paradox of music is that it's really meant to be played when you feel like playing it. It's not meant to be played like a job. The purest essence of music is an expression, it should be done like a painter. You don't paint when the audience comes in and pays their quarter. I don't think he did a good job of dealing with it. But it's understandable, considering how real he was."

all apologies

where did you sleep last night

nirvana closed out its *Unplugged* performance with a song by a writer Cobain referred to as "my favorite performer...our favorite performer" – Huddie Ledbetter, the seminal folk artist more often referred to as Leadbelly.

Ledbetter was a remarkable talent who was

The tunes of Huddie Ledbetter, aka Leadbelly, had a lasting influence on Cobain's writing.

"discovered" in the unlikeliest of places – the Louisiana State Penitentiary. In 1933, folk archivist John Lomax was traveling throughout the southern United States, making simple recordings of "found" music – work songs, back-porch blues, murder ballads and assorted folk tales. They had discovered that one of the richest sources of this kind of music was behind prison bars – prisoners who had little else to do but sing their songs to pass the time. In Louisiana, Lomax recognized a singular talent when he recorded several of Ledbetter's original songs. He went to the Louisiana governor and interceded on Ledbetter's behalf – the singer, who was in on a charge of attempted murder, was pardoned after he proved his worth by writing a song especially for the governor.

In the late 1930s, Ledbetter became a huge hit in the nightclubs of New York City and was one of the few black artists of the day who enjoyed widespread popularity with white audiences. An assault charge put a crimp in his career and sent him back to prison in 1939. But in 1940 he was thrilling crowds again, and working alongside such notable folk and blues singers as Woody Guthrie, Sonny Terry and Brownie McGhee. Leadbelly was at the peak of his abilities and popularity throughout most of the 1940s, penning such crowd-pleasing hits as 'Good Night, Irene', 'Rock Island Line' and 'In the Evening When the Sun Goes Down', while winning over working men and intelligentsia alike with his intensely funny, sharply observant political protest songs. Ledbetter had the foresight, or luck, to sit for a multitude of recording sessions. When he died of Lou Gehrig's

Dave Grohl would come out from behind the drums after Nirvana's demise and show off a variety of musical talents as the leader of the Foo Fighters.

disease in 1949, he left behind a treasure trove of recorded material.

Cobain got heavily into Leadbelly when he got hold of a copy of the two-volume set *Leadbelly's Last Sessions* while living in Olympia in 1988. Leadbelly's ability to combine simple words with just the right unexpected melodic turns and rhythms provided a lesson Cobain quickly took to heart and mastered in his own compositions. And Leadbelly remained an inspiration for him throughout Cobain's life – one he was eager to share with kindred spirits. When Cobain got to meet William S. Burroughs in late 1993 at Burroughs's home in Lawrence, Kansas, the gift the song writer gave to the author was a Leadbelly biography.

Cobain's first experience with 'Where Did You Sleep Last Night' – known alternately as 'In the Pines' – came about when he helped out his good friend Mark Lanegan of the Screaming Trees. (The singer was recording his first solo album, *The Winding Sheet*, for Sub Pop in 1990.) Lanegan and Cobain tried to write some original songs together, but when no great work seemed forthcoming they decided to record a couple of Leadbelly tunes. 'Where Did You Sleep Last Night' was recorded with Krist on bass, Kurt on

guitar, then-Screaming Trees-member Mark Pickerel on drums and Lanegan belting out the bloody tale of jealous suspicions. Cobain sang lead when the same bunch of musicians recorded a second Leadbelly tune, called 'Ain't It a Shame', but that track wasn't used on Lanegan's album and was never released as a single.

Cobain made an inspired choice in returning to 'Where Did You Sleep Last Night' as an *Unplugged* closer. The band was tight, the ominous cello lines are a beautiful touch and when Cobain's voice rockets raggedly into an upper register, as he growls out the final verses, it raises goosebumps and freezes the blood. Cobain was capable of great music on a regular basis, but in those few moments he worked magic.

"His version is the definitive version – it blows mine away," Lanegan told Jason Fine in an August 1996, *Rolling Stone* interview. "One of the coolest things that ever came from hanging with Kurt was just sitting in his shed and hearing him play acoustic guitar and singing. To me it sounded like what I imagined it would be like if I was sitting in the room with Skip James or Lightnin' Hopkins. It was so soulful and real, it gave me chills."

afterword

an interview with kurt cobain

After having heard much about Cobain's reputation as a smack-addled cipher ... I was very pleasantly surprised to find that he was warm, forthcoming, insightful...

I never got to meet Kurt Cobain, but I did have the opportunity to interview him, through a series of trans-Atlantic phone calls and faxes. In the months before his death, Kurt had been designing a guitar with the Fender Company (what came to be known as the 'Jag-stang' guitar – a custom-built Fender Jaguar, Fender Mustang hybrid). Kurt enjoyed his dealings with the company and had consequently agreed that he would, at some point, grant an interview for Fender's *Frontline* magazine. When I first contacted him to do that piece – in February 1994 – Nirvana was in Europe on what would be their final tour. Kurt was, somewhat understandably, less than eager to submit to interviews at the time, but it was made clear to him that the idea of the piece was not to prod him about any of the sensational rumors that were circulating about the band but to just let him speak frankly about his music. He graciously consented.

After having heard much about Cobain's reputation as a smack-addled cipher, egocentric brat and/or prickly press-hater, I was very pleasantly surprised to find that he was a warm, forthcoming, insightful and very funny interviewee. When our communications came to an end, I considered it a privilege to have made his acquaintance and wanted to make sure that the Cobain I had spoken with came through clearly in my piece. Unfortunately, before that piece had even been written, Kurt over-dosed on champagne and Rohypnol while the band was in Rome. This was, at first, described as an accident, but eventually it was revealed that it had been a calculated suicide attempt.

A month later, Cobain, having escaped from a rehabilitation facility in Los Angeles, made his way back to Seattle. On April 5, 1994, he barricaded himself in a room above his garage, put a shotgun to his head, and ended his life. After Cobain's death, the *Frontline* piece was re-edited, and what ran were excerpts from the following interview, along with a short memorial. Here is the full transcript of what was almost certainly one of Cobain's final interviews.

Q: Nirvana has become a "Big Rock Story", but the music still seems to be the most important part of that story. Your music offers the simple, powerful rock n' roll thrill that so many other bands seem to have a hard time delivering. How proud are you of Nirvana's work?

The music remains with us, but Kurt Cobain, and Nirvana, will be deeply missed.

KC: It's interesting, because while there's a certain selfish gratification in having any number of people buy your records and come to see you play, none of that holds a candle to simply hearing a song that I've written played by a band. I'm not talking about radio or MTV. I just really like playing these songs with a good drummer and bass player. Next to my wife and daughter, there's nothing that brings me more pleasure.

I'm extremely proud of what we've accomplished together. Having said that, however, I don't know how long we can continue as Nirvana without a radical shift in direction. I have lots of ideas and musical ambitions that have nothing to do with this mass conception of "grunge" that has been force-fed to the record-buying public for the past few years. Whether I will be able to do everything I want to do as part of Nirvana remains to be seen. To be fair, I also know that both Krist and Dave have musical ideas that may not work within the context of Nirvana. We're all tired of being labeled. You can't imagine how stifling it is.

Q: You've made it clear that you're not particularly comfortable being a "Rock Star", but one of the things that tracks like 'Heart-Shaped Box' and 'Pennyroyal Tea' on *In Utero* make clear is that you're certainly a gifted song writer. You may have a tough job sometimes, but has the writing process continued to be pleasurable and satisfying for you?

KC: I think it becomes less pleasurable and satisfying when I think of it in terms of being part of my "job." Writing is the one part that is not a job, it's expression. Photo shoots, interviews...that's the real job part.

Q: You're a very passionate performer. Do you find yourself re-experiencing the tenderness and the rage in your songs when you perform them?

KC: That's tough because the real core of any tenderness or rage is tapped the very second that a song is written. In a sense, I'm only re-creating the purity of that particular emotion every time I play that particular song. While it gets easier to summon those emotions with experience, it's a sort of dishonesty in that you can never recapture the emotion of a song completely each time you play it. Real "performing" implies a sort of acting that I've always tried to avoid.

Q: It must be a very odd feeling for Nirvana to be performing in sports arenas these days. How do you get along with the crowds you're attracting now?

KC: Much better than I used to. When we first started to get successful, I was extremely judgmental of the people in the audience. I held each of them to a sort of punk-rock ethos. It upset me that we were attracting and entertaining the very people that a lot of my music was a reaction against. I've since become much better at accepting people for who they are. Regardless of who they were before they came to the show, I get a few hours to try and subvert the way they view the world. It's not that I'm trying to dictate, it's just that I am afforded a certain platform on which I can express my views. At the very least, I always get the last word.

Q: There's a great deal of craft in your songs, but you also seem to enjoy the thrill of simply cranking up an electric guitar. Is playing guitar a pleasure for you, or do you battle with the instrument?

KC: The battle is the pleasure. I'm the anti-guitar hero – I can barely play the thing myself. I'm the first to admit that I'm no virtuoso. I can't play like Segovia. The flip side of that is that Segovia could probably never have played like me.

Q: With Pat Smear playing guitar in the touring line-up, has your approach to the instrument changed much? Is it easier to enjoy playing live with an extra pair of guitar-hands helping you out?

KC: Pat has worked out great from day one. In addition to being one of my closest friends, Pat has found a niche in our music that compliments what was already there, without forcing any major changes. While I don't see myself ever becoming Mick Jagger, having Pat on stage has freed me to spend more time concentrating on my connection with the audience. I've become more of a showman – well, maybe that's going too far. Let's just say that having Pat to hold down the rhythm allows me to concentrate on the performance as a whole. I think it's improved our live show 100%.

Q: On *In Utero*, and in concert, you play some of the most powerful "anti-solos" ever hacked out of a guitar. What comes to mind for you when it's time for the guitar to cut loose?

KC: Less than you could ever imagine.

Q: Krist and Dave do a great job of helping to bring your songs to life. How would you describe the role of each player, including yourself, in the Nirvana sound?

KC: While I can do a lot by switching channels on my amp, it's Dave who really brings the physicality to the dynamics in our songs. Krist is great at keeping everything going along at some kind of an even keel. I'm just the folk-singer in the middle.

Q: Aside from interviews, what are the biggest drags for you these days?

KC: Being apart from my family for months at a time. Having people feed me fine French meals when all I want is macaroni and cheese. Being seen as unapproachable when I used to just be called shy. Did I mention interviews?

Q: *Nevermind* changed your life in a big way, but having Courtney and Frances Bean around must help you keep things in perspective. How much do you enjoy being a family man?

KC: It's more important than anything else in the world. Playing music is what I do – my family is what I am. When everyone's forgotten about Nirvana and I'm on some revival tour opening for the Temptations and the Four Tops, Frances Bean will still be my daughter and Courtney will still be my wife. That means more than anything to me.

chronology

1965
May 16 Krist Anthony Novoselic is born in Compton, California.

1967
February 20 Kurt Donald Cobain is born in Hoquiam, Washington.

1969
January 14 David Eric Grohl is born in Warren, Ohio.

1985
Winter Kurt Cobain gets together with future Melvins drummer Dale Crover and friend Greg Hokanson. The short-lived trio is called Fecal Matter. They record a 4-track demo of Cobain originals, including one song 'Downer', that would later appear on *Bleach*.

December Marginally impressed with the Fecal Matter cassette, Krist Novoselic decides that he and Cobain should start a band. With an eye toward the money to be made in Aberdeen taverns, the two begin playing together as the Sellouts, a Creedence Clearwater Revival cover band.

1987
Winter After Novoselic returns from a period of residence in Arizona, he, Cobain and drummer Aaron Burckhard begin rehearsing. They perform as Skid Row, Bliss, Ted Ed Fred, Pen Cap Chew, Throat Oyster and Windowpane before settling on Nirvana.

April Cobain, Novoselic and Burckhard play as Nirvana on a radio show for KAOS, the station at Evergreen State College in Olympia, Washington. Among songs the band play are 'Love Buzz', 'Floyd the Barber', 'Mexican Seafood', 'Hairspray Queen' and 'Downer'.

1988
January 23 With drummer Dale Crover, Nirvana works through 10 songs at Reciprocal Studios in Seattle. Producer Jack Endino records and mixes the session. Three tracks from this session, 'Paper Cuts', 'Floyd the Barber' and 'Downer', will appear on *Bleach*.

February Endino passes a tape of the demos to Jonathan Poneman of Sub Pop records. Poneman loves the songs, though many he plays the tape for, including Sub Pop co-owner Bruce Pavitt, are not as impressed. He pursues the band, and gets them interested in doing a single for Sub Pop.

Spring The band rehearses and performs with Dale Crover, Aaron Burckhard and Dave Foster before deciding to recruit Chad Channing as Nirvana's drummer.

June-July The band has several sessions to record its first single for Sub Pop records.

November Sub Pop releases the first Nirvana single, 'Love Buzz'/'Big Cheese'.

December Nirvana begins sessions with Jack Endino at Reciprocal Studios for the tracks that will make up their first album, *Bleach*.

1989
February Nirvana becomes a quartet with the addition of guitarist Jason Everman. Everman does not play on *Bleach*, but puts up the money for its recording. The band begins a West Coast tour.

June 15 *Bleach* is released on Sub Pop. The group begins its first extensive US tour. The tour is cut short because of conflicts with Everman. When the band returns to Seattle, Everman is no longer a member of Nirvana.

August The band records its 'Blew' EP sessions with producer Steve Fisk at Music Source studios in Seattle.

October 20 Nirvana embarks on its first European tour, with label-mates TAD.

December 30 Krist Novoselic marries his long-time girlfriend Shelli in their Tacoma apartment.

1990
January-March The band plays gigs throughout California and the Northwest US.

April The band spends a week recording demo sessions at Smart Studios in Madison, Wisconsin, with producer Butch Vig. Among recorded tracks are 'In Bloom', 'Dive', 'Lithium' and the version of 'Polly' that would end up on *Nevermind*.

May The band undertakes its second major US tour. At the end of the tour, Kurt and Krist fire Chad Channing. Dale Crover fills in for a seven-date West Coast tour.

July 11 The band records 'Sliver' with producer Jack Endino. Mudhoney's Dan Peters plays drums on the track.

September 22 Nirvana, with Peters on drums, headlines a major show at the Motor Sports International and Garage in Seattle. Dave Grohl is in the audience.

October After a quick audition, Dave Grohl is welcomed

into Nirvana. The new line-up takes off for a brief tour of Britain.

December 1 Sub Pop releases the 'Sliver'/'Dive' single. Nirvana is using its Smart sessions demos to generate major label interest.

1991

April 30 Nirvana formally signs on with Geffen Records.

May-June Nirvana temporarily relocates to Los Angeles and records the tracks for *Nevermind* at Sound City studios in Van Nuys, California, with Butch Vig producing. During these sessions, a relationship begins between Cobain and Courtney Love.

June Nirvana opens for Dinosaur Jr. on a West Coast mini-tour.

August 20 Nirvana plays nine dates across Europe, including a triumphant set at the Reading Festival.

September 13 A *Nevermind* release party is held at Re-bar in Seattle. It comes to a messy end when the members of Nirvana instigate a full-scale food fight.

September 20 The band embarks on a six-week tour of the US and Canada.

September 24 Geffen Records releases *Nevermind*. Its first pressing calls for less than 50,000 copies. By Christmas, the album is selling 400,000 copies a week.

October 25 Nirvana tapes a segment for MTV's *Headbanger's Ball*. 'Smells Like Teen Spirit' is the program's "Skullcrusher of the Week."

November 2 The band sets out on a European tour.

December Nirvana tours briefly with Pearl Jam and the Red Hot Chilli Peppers.

1992

January 11 *Nevermind* is the Number One record on the Billboard album charts.

January 24 Nirvana tours California, Australia, New Zealand, Japan and Hawaii.

February 24 Kurt Cobain marries Courtney Love in Hawaii.

May Cobain checks into Exodus, a drug rehabilitation program in Los Angeles, for treatment of his heroin addiction. He leaves the program before his treatment is finished.

June The band tours Ireland, Northern Ireland, Scandinavia, France and Spain.

August *Vanity Fair* publishes an article insinuating that Courtney Love is an unfit, heroin-addicted mother-to-be.

August 18 Frances Bean Cobain is born in Los Angeles. Kurt Cobain is de-toxing at the same hospital. Child welfare authorities revoke the Cobains' custody of their child. The case isn't settled until March, 1993.

August 30 Making a joke of the (accurate) rumors of his ill health, Kurt is brought to the stage of the Reading Festival in a hospital smock and wheelchair. Nirvana's head-lining set is ecstatically received.

September 9 Nirvana plays the MTV Video Music Awards. The band wishes to play 'Rape Me' but are asked not to by MTV staff. Cobain plays the opening

bars of the song before the band breaks into 'Lithium'. Backstage, the Cobains and Axl Rose exchange unpleasant words, and Kurt and Axl engage in a shoving match.

September 11 Nirvana plays a Seattle benefit for the Washington Music Industry Coalition, an anti-censorship group.

December 15 *Incesticide* is released.

1993

January Nirvana, with L7, play two large stadium shows in São Paolo and Rio de Janeiro, Brazil.

February The band has recording sessions for *In Utero* at Pachyderm Studios in Minnesota with producer Steve Albini.

March The Cobains buy two homes in the Seattle area – a lakeside home in the city itself, and an estate in Carnation.

March 23 The legal battles over Frances Bean come to an end, with the charges against Kurt and Courtney being rendered not legally valid.

April 9 Nirvana plays a benefit at the Cow Palace in San Francisco, on a bill with L7, the Breeders and Disposable Heroes of Hiphoprisy. They raise money for the Tresnjevka Women's Group, a Croatian organization assisting rape victims in the war-torn region.

May 2 Cobain suffers a heroin overdose in Seattle and is hospitalized.

May 17 *Newsweek* magazine runs an article on the "controversy" behind the *In Utero* tracks that have been submitted to Geffen. A great deal of subsequent press focuses on the odd, three-way conflict of opinion between Nirvana, Steve Albini and Geffen as to the way the recording sessions went and the quality of the music made.

September 21 *In Utero* is released and debuts as the Number One album on the *Billboard* charts.

October 18 Nirvana embarks on an extensive US tour. Pat Ruthensmear is added as a second guitarist.

November 18 Nirvana, in New York, plays the "unplugged" set that will be released the following year as an album.

January 7-8 Nirvana plays its final US shows, at the Seattle Center Arena.

February 2 Nirvana begins a European tour.

March 1 The band gives what will be its final performance at Terminal Einz, Munich.

March 4 Cobain overdoses in Rome on a combination of champagne and Rohypnol. Nirvana management at first claim that this is an accident. Later it is clear that it was a suicide attempt.

March 30 Cobain spends two days at the Exodus rehabilitation center in Los Angeles.

April 1 Cobain scales a wall to escape Exodus, and flies to Seattle.

April 5 In a room over the garage of his Seattle home at 171 Lake Washington Blvd. E., Kurt Cobain writes a suicide note, gives himself a heroin injection and then ends his life with a shotgun blast to the head.

discography

UK singles and eps

'Blew' *December, 1989, Tupelo EP8/CDB*

'Blew'/'Love Buzz'/'Been A Son'/'Stain'

'Sliver'/'Dive' *January, 1991, Tupelo, TUP 25*

'Sliver'/'Dive'/'About A Girl' (Live) *April, 1991, Tupelo EP25/CD25*

'Smells Like Teen Spirit'/'Drain You' *August, 1991, DGC 5*

'Smells Like Teen Spirit'/'Even In His Youth'/'Aneurysm' *September 9, 1991, DGCCD 5*

'Smells Like Teen Spirit'/'Even In His Youth'/'Aneurysm'/'Drain You' *November, 1991, DGCTD 5*

'Come As You Are'/'Endless, Nameless' *March 1, 1992, DGC 7*

'Come As You Are'/'Endless, Nameless'/'School' (Live) *March, 1992, DGCTD 7*

'Come As You Are'/ 'School' (Live)/'Drain You' (live) *March, 1992, DGCS 7*

'Lithium'/'Curmudgeon' *July 9, 1992, DGCS 9*

'Lithium'/'Been A Son' (Live)/'Curmudgeon' *July 20, 1992, DGCSD 9*

'In Bloom'/'Polly' (Live) *November, 1992, Geffen GFS 34*

'In Bloom'/'Sliver' (Live)/'Polly' (Live) *November 1992, Geffen GFSTD 34*

'Oh, The Guilt'/ b/w 'Puss' (by the Jesus Lizard) *February, 1993, Touch&Go TG83*

'Heart-Shaped Box'/'Marigold' (written and sung by Dave Grohl) *August, 1993, Geffen GFS 54*

'Heart-Shaped Box'/'Milk It'/'Marigold' (written and sung by Dave Grohl) *September, 1993, Geffen GFSTD 54*

'All Apologies'/'Rape Me' *December 1993, Geffen GFS 66*

albums

Bleach *August 1989, Tupelo TUP LP 6/MC 6/ CD 6* 'Blew'; 'Floyd the Barber'; 'About A Girl'; 'School'; 'Love Buzz'; 'Paper Cuts'; 'Negative Creep'; 'Scoff'; 'Swap Meet'; 'Mr. Moustache'; 'Sifting'. **Re-issued in April 1992**, *Geffen GEF 24433* Additional tracks: 'Big Cheese'; 'Downer'.

Nevermind *September 1991, Geffen DGC 24425* 'Smells Like Teen Spirit'; 'In Bloom'; 'Come As You Are'; 'Breed'; 'Lithium'; 'Polly'; 'Territorial Pissings'; 'Drain You'; 'Lounge Act'; 'Stay Away'; 'On a Plain'; 'Something In the Way'; 'Endless, Nameless'.

Incesticide *December 14 1992, Geffen GEF 24504* 'Dive'; 'Sliver'; 'Stain'; 'Been A Son'; 'Turnaround'; 'Molly's Lips'; 'Son of a Gun'; '(New Wave)Polly'; 'Beeswax'; 'Downer'; 'Mexican Seafood'; 'Hairspray Queen'; 'Aero Zeppelin'; 'Big Long Now'; 'Aneurysm'.

In Utero *September 13, 1993, Geffen GEF 24536* 'Serve the Servants'; 'Scentless Apprentice'; 'Heart-Shaped Box'; 'Rape Me'; 'Frances Farmer Will Have Her Revenge On Seattle'; 'Dumb'; 'Very Ape'; 'Milk It'; 'Pennyroyal Tea'; 'Radio Friendly Unit Shifter'; 'Tourette's'; 'All Apologies'; 'Gallons of Rubbing Alcohol Flow Through the Strip'.

Unplugged in New York *October 1994, Geffen GEF 24727* 'About A Girl'; 'Come As You Are'; 'Jesus Doesn't Want Me For A Sunbeam'; 'The Man Who Sold the World'; 'Pennyroyal Tea'; 'Dumb'; 'Polly'; 'On a Plain'; 'Something In the Way'; 'Plateau'; 'Oh Me'; 'Lake of Fire'; 'All Apologies'; 'Where Did You Sleep Last Night'.

From the Muddy Banks of Wishkah *October 8, 1996 Geffen* 16 tracks from live performances 1989–1994.

US singles and eps

'Love Buzz'/'Big Cheese' *November 1988, Sub Pop SP 23*

'Blew' *December, 1989, Tupelo EP8/CDB*

'Blew'/'Love Buzz'/'Been A Son'/'Stain'

'Sliver'/'Dive' *September 1990, Sub Pop SP 73*

'Molly's Lips'/'Candy' (by the Fluid) *April 1991, Sub Pop Singles Club number 27*

'Here She Comes Now' (Nirvana cover of Velvet Underground song)**/'Venus in Furs'** (Melvins cover of Velvet Underground song) *June 1991, Communion*

Records, Communion 23

'Smells Like Teen Spirit'/'Even In His Youth'/'Aneurysm' *September 9, 1991, DGCCD 5*

'Come As You Are'/'School' (Live)/'Drain You' (live) *March, 1992, DGCS 7*

'Lithium'/'Been A Son' (Live)/'Curmudgeon' *July 20, 1992, DGCSD 9*

'Oh, The Guilt'/ b/w 'Puss' (by the Jesus Lizard) *February, 1993, Touch&Go TG83*

albums

Bleach *June 1989, Sub Pop SP 34* 'Blew'; 'Floyd the Barber'; 'About A Girl'; 'School'; 'Love Buzz'; 'Paper Cuts'; 'Negative Creep'; 'Scoff'; 'Swap Meet'; 'Mr. Moustache'; 'Sifting'. **Re-issued in April** 1992, *Geffen GEF 24433* Additional tracks: 'Big Cheese'; 'Downer'.

Nevermind *September 1991, Geffen DGC 24425* 'Smells Like Teen Spirit'; 'In Bloom'; 'Come As You Are'; 'Breed'; 'Lithium'; 'Polly'; 'Territorial Pissings'; 'Drain You'; 'Lounge Act'; 'Stay Away'; 'On a Plain'; 'Something In the Way'; 'Endless, Nameless'.

Incesticide *December 14 1992, Geffen GEF 24504* 'Dive'; 'Sliver'; 'Stain'; 'Been A Son'; 'Turnaround'; 'Molly's Lips'; 'Son of a Gun'; '(New Wave) Polly'; 'Beeswax'; 'Downer'; 'Mexican Seafood'; 'Hairspray Queen'; 'Aero Zeppelin'; 'Big Long Now'; 'Aneurysm'.

In Utero *September 13, 1993, Geffen GEF 24536* 'Serve the Servants'; 'Scentless Apprentice'; 'Heart-Shaped Box'; 'Rape Me'; 'Frances Farmer Will Have Her Revenge On Seattle'; 'Dumb'; 'Very Ape'; 'Milk It'; 'Pennyroyal Tea'; Radio Friendly Unit Shifter'; 'Tourette's'; 'All Apologies'; 'Gallons of Rubbing Alcohol Flow Through the Strip'.

Unplugged in New York *October 1994, Geffen GEF 24727* 'About A Girl'; 'Come As You Are'; 'Jesus Doesn't Want Me For A Sunbeam'; 'The Man Who Sold the World'; 'Pennyroyal Tea'; 'Dumb'; 'Polly'; 'On a Plain'; 'Something In the Way'; 'Plateau'; 'Oh Me'; 'Lake of Fire'; All Apologies'; 'Where Did You Sleep Last Night'.

From the Muddy Banks of Wishkah *October 8, 1996 Geffen* 16 tracks from live performances 1989–1994.

compilations and related recordings

'Spank Thru' *Sub Pop 200*, compilation *December, 1988, Sub Pop SP25*

'Bikini Twilight' by the Go Team (Calvin Johnson and Tobi Vail, featuring Kurt Cobain) *July 1989, K Records*

'Mexican Seafood' *Teriyaki Asthma, Vol. 1*, compilation *November, 1989, C/Z Records, CZ037*

'Where Did You Sleep Last Night' (featuring Kurt Cobain and Krist Novoselic)

The Winding Sheet, Mark Lanegan (Screaming Trees) solo album *May 1990, Sub Pop, SP61*

'Do You Love Me' (w/Jason Everman in line-up) *Hard To Believe,* Kiss tribute album *August 1990, C/Z Records, CZ024*

'Here She Comes Now' *Heaven and Hell Vol. 1*, Velvet Underground tribute album *June 1991, Communion Records, Communion 20*

'Beeswax' *Kill Rock Stars,* compilation *August 21, 1991, Kill Rock Stars, KRS 201*

'Bureaucratic Desire for Revenge' EP by Earth (featuring Kurt Cobain) *October 1991, Sub Pop, SP 123*

'Return of the Rat' *Eight Songs for Greg Sage and the Wipers,* tribute album *June 20, 1992, Tim Kerr Records, T/K 917010 TRIB 2*

'The Priest, They Called Him' by William S. Burroughs, featuring Kurt Cobain *July 1993, Tim Kerr Records, T/K 9210044/92CD044*

'I Hate Myself and Want to Die' *The Beavis and Butt-head Experience,* compilation *1993, Geffen, GEFD 24613*

'Houdini' The Melvins, produced by Kurt Cobain *1993, Atlantic*

'Verse Chorus Verse' *No Alternative,* compilation *1993, Arista*

'Pay to Play' *DGC Rarities Vol. 1,* compilation *1994, Geffen*

index